The Massey Lectures Series

The Massey Lectures are co-sponsored by Massey College, in the University of Toronto, and CBC Radio. The series was created in honour of the Right Honourable Vincent Massey, former governor general of Canada, and was inaugurated in 1961 to enable distinguished authorities to communicate the results of original study or research on subjects of contemporary interest.

This book comprises the 1997 Massey Lectures, "The Elsewhere Community," broadcast in November 1997 as part of CBC Radio's *Ideas* series. The producer of the series was Sara Wolch; the executive producer was Bernie Lucht.

Hugh Kenner

Hugh Kenner is the Fuller E. Callaway Professor of English and Franklin Professor in the College of Arts and Sciences at the University of Georgia. Originally from Peterborough, Ontario, he has been ranked with Northrop Frye and Marshall McLuhan as one of the finest critics to come out of Canada. He is a fellow of the Royal Society of Literature and he has held the Northrop Frye Chair at the University of Toronto. His thirty-plus books include studies of T. S. Eliot, Samuel Beckett, James Joyce, and his definitive work on Ezra Pound, entitled *The Pound Era*. His writing encompasses the fields of literature, language, art, history, mathematics, computer programming, and popular culture.

ALSO BY HUGH KENNER

Paradox in Chesterton, 1948
The Poetry of Ezra Pound, 1951
Wyndham Lewis, 1954
Dublin's Joyce, 1956
Gnomon: Essays in Contemporary Literature, 1958
The Invisible Poet: T. S. Eliot, 1958
The Art of Poetry, 1959
Seventeenth-Century Poetry: The Schools of Donne and Jonson
    (editor), 1965
Samuel Beckett: A Critical Study, 1961
The Stoic Comedians, 1963
The Counterfeiters, 1968
The Pound Era, 1971
Bucky: A Guided Tour of Buckminster Fuller, 1973
A Reader's Guide to Samuel Beckett, 1973
A Homemade World: The American Modernist Writers, 1975
Geodesic Math and How to Use It, 1976
Joyce's Voices, 1978
Ulysses, 1982
A Colder Eye: The Modern Irish Writers, 1983
The Mechanic Muse, 1987
A Sinking Island: The Modern Irish Writers, 1988
Mazes, 1989
Historical Fictions, 1990
Chuck Jones: A Flurry of Drawings, 1994

HUGH KENNER

THE ELSEWHERE COMMUNITY

First published in 1998 by
House of Anansi Press Limited
1800 Steeles Avenue West
Concord, Ontario
L4K 2P3
Tel. (416) 445-3333
Fax (416) 445-5967

02 01 00 99 98 1 2 3 4 5

CBC logo used by permission

Canadian Cataloguing in Publication Data

Kenner, Hugh, 1923–
The elsewhere community
(CBC Massey lectures series)
ISBN 0-88784-607-6

1. Civilization, Western.   I. Title.   II. Series.

CB69.K46   1998   909.8   C97-931864-5

Cover Design: Bill Douglas at The Bang
Text Design: Tannice Goddard

Printed in Canada

*House of Anansi Press gratefully acknowledges the support of
the Canada Council for the Arts and the Ontario Arts Council in the
development of writing and publishing in Canada.*

For Christopher

Contents

I

REFLECTIONS ON THE GRAND TOUR

MY FATHER (BORN IN 1867) and my mother (born in 1882) each visited Europe once. That seems to have been normal for educated Canadians of their generation. When I was growing up in Peterborough, the one man I knew who had been to Europe more than once — three or four times, I think — owned a prosperous business. My parents were teachers, and in their day, high school teachers were expected to have been to Europe. My French teacher had been to Europe once, some decades after my parents. So had my German teacher, and I think my Latin teacher as well. But once was all they could afford. They crossed the Atlantic by steamship and then got about by train.

I first visited Europe, by air, in 1956. I was thirty-three years old. I have no idea how many times I've been there since: dozens, certainly. That does not reflect any affluence of mine, but rather, the incredibly low cost of transatlantic travel once airports rather than harbours began dominating it. College kids I meet now take for granted a "European tour" — or even an "Oriental tour" — between terms, on a shoestring. Once they're home, they feel sure they'll be going back again.

In my parents' day, continental Europe was considered foreign, though the British Isles were not. After all, English-speaking Canada had been so recently settled from those Isles. The British North America Act, which created the Dominion of Canada, came into effect in 1867; so England, for my father who was born there in that year, was "the Old Country." And though my mother was born in Ontario, her own mother was Scottish and her father Welsh. Wales and Scotland and England were not "abroad"; they were emotionally close, even though it cost about as much to get to Britain as to Europe, involving as they each did that Atlantic crossing.

But it was after you arrived in Britain, when you confronted merely crossing the Channel, that the true journey abroad began: your tour of "the continent." In the first part of this century, there was such curiosity among Canadians about Europe that the *Peterborough Review* (the local newspaper) published a series of articles by my father about his travels there. The offprints were later gathered into a rare little book called *A Trip to the Eternal City*. Let me quote from a line or two:

> The very dust of Rome's streets, the soil of her suburbs, has for the reflective mind a solemn interest. That dust

once lived, jested and hated, toiled and battled. Some atoms of that soil made Cicero's lips of eloquence and Caesar's brain of power: all shrivelled and withered now into a few handfuls of wind-driven dust.[1]

"All humans, by their nature," said Aristotle, "desire to know."[2] A special and unparalleled way to know is to go where you've never been. And the key to this quest for knowledge is "elsewhere." In going there, you join what, in these lectures, we will be calling an "Elsewhere Community." It's a concept that is impossible to define strictly. It can name where you dream of going — where bluebirds fly, perhaps. Or it can describe the people you've met somewhere, memories of whom have helped to change you. Or it's an awareness of your own growth and change, arising from the places you've been: Rome's Sistine Chapel, perhaps, or the Zen Gardens of Kyoto, or the green oasis of Manhattan's Central Park.

For my father, a journey to Rome meant encounters with experiences — elsewhere — which helped him to enrich his community back home. And what he was doing by going there, what my teachers and my students were doing, and what I myself have done is to re-enact a long-standing tradition: the Grand Tour.

It became standardized in the eighteenth century. Members of the British upper class — especially young men with time and money — began touring the continent. You crossed the Channel, which in choppy weather could itself be an adventure — "Rough passage, and arrived . . . in a piteous condition,"[3] wrote a twenty-year-old passenger in 1780. And then Paris: "The clearness of the air, the glittering sunshine,"[4] exclaimed William Hazlitt, a refugee from London mists who went on to marvel at the view through the Tuileries archway at the end of the Champs Elysées — "the effect is exquisitely light and magical."[5] He contrasted Paris with the look of London: "like a long black wreath of smoke, with the dome of St. Paul's floating in it."[6] Next, perhaps, it was off to mountainous Switzerland: to Geneva, where there could be found many streets "far more agreeable to descend than to climb,"[7] as one American wrote. But whatever the route, the major destination was always Rome.

To get to Italy from France you had to cross the Alps. It's easy now; I've actually dozed through it on a midday train. But three centuries ago, the Alpine crossing was a misery. One traveller remembered arriving on the Italian side "half starved with cold and hunger."[8] He'd been carried sitting in a chair suspended from poles which four to eight men had borne on their shoulders. It seems never to have occurred to these young and robust Anglos that walking the twelve miles or so might have been easier. His party's baggage went on mules, as did pieces of a carriage that would be assembled once the mountains lay behind.

For Grand Tourists, it's clear that the Alps were an obstacle, not a pleasure, and accounts of the crossing are devoid of rapture. Yet beyond the Alps lay what, for many Englishmen, the Grand Tour was all about. Though no man is an island, Britain inescapably was one, and having qualified at Oxford or Cambridge for the civilized life, the young eighteenth-century Briton ideally would complete his education where civilization was held to have begun. For had he not started his education with the study of Latin?

London's principal sage in those years, Dr. Samuel Johnson — unhandsome, half-blind, garrulous, and responsible for the celebrated *Dictionary of the English Language* — said that a man who has not been to Italy is always conscious of an inferiority "from his not having seen what it is expected a man should see."[9] (It's worth remarking that Johnson himself never had the means to see Italy.) And what was it "expected" that people should see? One traveller recalled the Colosseum by moonlight, and the interior of St Peter's Basilica: "all airy magnificence and gigantic splendour."[10] For the novelist Stendhal, in 1819, Michelangelo's *Last Judgement* on the Sistine Chapel ceiling fully made up for the "daemonic caterwauling" of the choir.[11] Edward Gibbon, however, who later wrote the monumental *History of the Decline and Fall of the Roman Empire*, put the matter best. Recalling a night in his twenties when he was sleepless from excitement, he extols the ruins of the Roman Forum, "where Romulus stood, or Tully spoke, or Caesar fell."[12] Romulus was a cofounder of Rome; Tully was Cicero, history's greatest orator; Caesar, on the verge of the great Empire, was murdered. And only one square of space evoked those memories. Gibbon had brought to Rome, in his mind, much that the Elsewhere Community would flesh out.

In finding Rome, a traveller such as Gibbon had found himself. Who am I, what are my roots? You can see Gibbon's person, his education, his aptitudes, all coming together in

Rome. The result was a centred Gibbon, who would make a lifetime's work producing the greatest historical work in the English language. "It was at Rome," he wrote, "on the fifteenth of October 1764, as I sat musing amidst the ruins of the Capitol, while the barefoot friars were singing vespers in the Temple of Jupiter, that the idea of writing the decline and fall of the city first started in my mind."[13]

On the Grand Tour you could learn both of the world and of yourself. For in Rome, as the German poet Goethe put it, you learn to

> See with an eye that can feel, feel with a hand that
>   can see.[14]

Ideally, the traveller saw the sights his education had prepared him for, and the sights in turn extended his education. There were groups that travelled with tutors, and there were individuals who carried letters of introduction to prominent citizens abroad. These citizens — artists, for instance, or aristocrats, or authorities on history — could be the best discoveries of one's tour. Here where they lived, they could supply a few words of explanation that could help you become oriented with a city, a culture.

And so you might arrive in Milan and see Leonardo da Vinci's *Last Supper* — nowadays, to fulfil memories based on a reproduction — only to confront a disappointing mess. An on-the-spot informant could quickly clear that up: it's been falling apart and undergoing restoration almost since it was made, because da Vinci carelessly experimented with painting in oil over a wet wall meant for fresco. Such an explanation permits you to see past the dismal surface to the incredible power of the composition: the apostles in agitated groups of three; Judas isolated among them by his dark, defiant profile. The explanation is essential. An eighteenth-century traveller's best resource would be just such an informant, should he have a letter to one. Remember, there were no art books with photographic illustrations. Today, such a work may have enlightened you before leaving home; or perhaps you make do with your pocket guidebook. Either way, you have the means of discerning what da Vinci had in mind.

And so, we're back to Aristotle, reminding us how all humans by their nature desire to know. And what we don't know yet, what we don't know here, is to be found Elsewhere.

Earlier than the Grand Tour, even earlier than Aristotle, at the very dawn of Western history, we find the idea that a journey is in some way linked to what we hope to know. Nearly 3,000 years ago, in about the ninth century B.C., the poet Homer was implying that all people share a desire to travel, and therefore a love of hearing about travel. His epic poem *The Odyssey* is the story of a journey: the tale of a man named Odysseus whose simple wish is to get home, and of the delays, year after year, that keep him from getting there.

Odysseus was the king of Ithaca and the cleverest of the Greeks. He'd gone off to fight in the Trojan War, and after ten years, when the war was over, he set sail for home. The voyage should have taken a few weeks; it took ten more years. What was it that was delaying him? The Lord of the Sea, as Odysseus well knew. But what he didn't know was what he could do in order to get back home.

Within *The Odyssey* we find the story of a second journey. A supernatural being named Circe — a female magician — tells Odysseus that the only way to get around the Sea God and get back home is by travelling to the Far Shore where dwell the Dead. Once there, he must consult the ghost of a sage named Tiresias. And so Odysseus undertakes a journey after knowledge, fuelled by his desire to get home. The knowledge he acquires turns out to be his means of finally getting home. For to travel is always, in some sense, to learn. What we don't know yet, is to be found Elsewhere.

I want to continue with that idea: people travelling after what they do not know. Such a pursuit is a way of seeking entrance to the Elsewhere Community. The examples I use to illustrate this journey will be literary, because literature is what I know.

And literary examples abound. Thus an Irish poet named Paddy Kavanagh, born in 1904 in a place called Mucker (if you can believe it), walked at age twenty-seven, the entire fifty-five miles from Mucker southward to Dublin, begging his bread en route, just so he could drop in on a man he'd never met but whose writing had piqued his curiosity. That was a poet named George William Russell, who was then more than twice Paddy's age. He was hardly qualified to help Paddy improve his writing, since the poems he'd long been publishing under the mysterious pseudonym "AE" were just about as vaguely worded as Paddy's:

Now the quietude of earth
Nestles deep my heart within.[15]

That's AE; here's Paddy:

I find a star-lovely art
In a dark sod . . .[16]

If Paddy hadn't supposed that writing became poetic by
being vague he'd likely not have been drawn to AE in the
first place. But AE had more to offer Paddy than a limp
example. He was to go home lugging sixty odd pounds of
books from AE's shelves: books he'd never have read on
the farm in Mucker, books by the likes of the French novelist Victor Hugo and the American poet Walt Whitman. In
reading the books, in remembering AE's talk and his hospitality, Paddy would slowly make that community — that
Elsewhere Community — a part of himself. Later, in Dublin,
he'd share it with other folk, many of them younger than
he'd been when he'd made the journey. And by the time
Paddy died in Dublin at sixty-three, the examples of clean,
clear, unpretentious writing he left behind, in part thanks
to those books, would point a direction for a whole generation of young Irish writers. The Nobel Prizewinning poet
Seamus Heaney, for instance, has stated that reading
Paddy Kavanagh was what made him think he might have
something to write about, himself. And James Joyce was
even known to have written, "A.E.I.O.U."[17] So much would
emerge from one farmboy's 1931 walk, Mucker to Dublin
and back.

A second example comes from my own, personal

experience. On my first trip to France, in 1958, I had hoped to meet Samuel Beckett, then famous chiefly as the author of *Waiting for Godot*. The friend who'd given me Beckett's Paris address warned me of a problem: while mail piled up unanswered, Sam dithered and postponed out of a feeling that he ought to start at the bottom of the pile. On the plane from Montreal, a French detective novel gave me an idea for getting around that pile. At any post office in Paris in those days you could ask for a "pneumatique." The clerk would push what looked like an Air Letter form towards you; you'd write your message, seal it, watch the form go into a brass cylinder, then drop down a pneumatic tube. It then zoomed through the famous sewers of Paris, and at the post office nearest the address it was handed to a boy who bicycled to the addressee, knocked, handed the message over, and asked if there would be a reply. I tried it, and it worked. Within hours Samuel Beckett and I were in touch.

From that day on, we were friends for thirty years. He was the sweetest man I've ever known. He was also my model, whenever I was writing, for the discipline of utter economy: start with short words, progress in short, clear increments. And elegance comes less from ornament than from spareness.

At our last meeting, three months before his death, he confided that there was no longer a pneumatique.

Samuel Beckett wrote in French; though, of course, having been born in Ireland, he spoke beautifully economical English. I also spoke some French, so fortunately we had no trouble communicating. But foreign travel can open linguistic chasms. That was a recurring problem with the Grand Tour. True, there were some who learned chiefly the delights of Italian sensuality. Other travellers, though, were qualified for some encounter that would leave its mark; might even leave a mark on a book we still read. John Milton's *Paradise Lost* is such a book. It was published as long ago as 1667, and has become one of the most influential books in the English language.

When he was thirty years old, many years before he'd begun work on his major poem, John Milton set off on his own Grand Tour, chiefly to Italy. In Florence, he met Galileo, then seventy-four and under house arrest for affirming a heresy: that all the planets, including earth, revolve around the sun. Galileo's interest in the heavens began when he was thirty-five. He had heard a rumour about someone in Belgium having invented a gadget that made distant objects seem nearer. Galileo then assembled some lenses on his own, and managed a three-times magnification. Eventually, with much work shaping and reshaping the lenses, he raised the magnification level to thirty-three. Turning his telescopes on the skies, he discovered wonders: four satellites around Jupiter, spots on the sun, and — what seems to have most impressed young Milton — mountains and valleys on the moon.

Years later, Milton opened *Paradise Lost* with the angels who rebelled against God and were cast out of Heaven to fall nine long days into a burning lake. After another nine days of recuperation, their leader — the arch-fiend Satan — made for the shore. Milton describes his stance:

> his ponderous shield . . .
> Hung on his shoulders like the Moon, whose Orb
> Through Optic Glass the Tuscan Artist views
> At Ev'ning from the top of Fesole,
> Or in Valdarno, to descry new Lands,
> Rivers or Mountains in her spotty Globe.[18]

The "Tuscan Artist" is Galileo, whom Milton had visited years before in Florence, the capital of Tuscany. He remembered Galileo as the first human to have seen, with the aid of his Optic Glass, lunar features till then unguessed at — if not "Rivers," certainly "Mountains." Valdarno is the valley of the river Arno, which flows through Florence; and Fesole, where Milton imagined him observing, is a little hill overlooking Florence. In verse written years after his visit with Galileo, Milton is remembering the exact details of his visit; he'd been thirty, Galileo seventy-four, and their relationship, therefore, one of student and mentor.

It's notable, moreover, that the *Paradise Lost* of Milton, himself a journeyer, ends with the first of all journeys, that of Adam and Eve once Paradise has been closed. Here are Milton's sonorous final lines:

> Some natural tears they dropp'd, but wip'd them soon;
> The World was all before them, where to choose
> Thir place of rest, and Providence thir guide:
> They hand in hand with wand'ring steps and slow,
> Through Eden took thir solitary way.[19]

"The World was all before them": how that sentence will echo and re-echo throughout subsequent writing in English! A century or so later, in 1795, we find the poet William Wordsworth discerning an Elsewhere Community of his own in Milton's *Paradise Lost*. Wordsworth had been set free from the city of London by a legacy. Hear him, in his autobiographical poem, *The Prelude*, recollecting in tranquillity how he felt at twenty-five:

> The earth is all before me. With a heart
> Joyous, nor scared at its own liberty,
> I look about . . .[20]

"The earth is all before me": put that beside the Milton passage and it echoes; interactions crowd upon the mind. The world before them, even all of it, is a dubious compensation for Adam and Eve, who will never be in earthly Paradise again. But for Wordsworth, the earth all before him is unambiguous opportunity; it is joy, it is adventure.

Moreover, Wordsworth's escape from London suggests another influential passage from *Paradise Lost*. The first act of Milton's fallen angels, on emerging from the burning lake of Hell, is to build themselves a huge city, "Pandaemonium, the high Capitol / Of Satan and his Peers."[21] It exuded unimaginable luxury, all of it pagan. From then on, Milton's readers could not help but map that city back onto their own familiar world. An England of the imagination was permanently altered. The old interplay of pastoral and urban, country and town, each with its fitting virtues, was converted into something sinister: the city as

Satan's invention, a model of Pandaemonium. From then on, British imaginations would contrast an "idyllic country" with an "infernal city," chiefly represented by London. For Wordsworth, and later for Charles Dickens and Sir Arthur Conan Doyle, the city is a corrupting place indeed. In London, Doyle suggests, the police may do their fumbling best, but without Sherlock Holmes what might life in that crime-ridden ferment be?

So there's Wordsworth, age twenty-five, hating London and rejoicing to be free from it, with a nod to Milton. Again and again in *The Prelude* Wordsworth uses *Paradise Lost* in this way, paying Milton the compliment of never identifying him. For will not his readers detect Milton's presence in a single borrowed phrase?

Wordsworth's easy familiarity with *Paradise Lost* confers new inflections on the notion of an Elsewhere Community. For it's clear that when he inserts Miltonic turns of phrase into *The Prelude*, he isn't appropriating goodies, something nervous writers do when they can hope they'll not be detected. Nor, on the other hand, does he imagine he's showing Milton up. No, in an almost unique relationship, Wordsworth and Milton inhabit, in comfort, the "community of English poetry," a community their readers will also appreciate. When Wordsworth was preparing to enter that community, Milton was a part of his education. Now he can assume that he and Milton together are part of ours.

And Wordsworth, by the end of the eighteenth century, was an English poet's model for large-scale effects. Let's consider how he handles an incident of his own Grand Tour: his crossing of the Alps in 1790. Wordsworth was not carried in a chair suspended on poles; he crossed on foot. The crossing itself was anticlimactic: no hours of cold and starvation, no luggage tumbling downhill. No, amid much mutual misunderstanding with a helpful peasant, he and his companion came to realize that there'd be no more upwardness because they'd crossed the Alpine saddle unbeknownst to them and were now on the descent.

> Loth to believe what we so grieved to hear,
> For still we had hopes that pointed to the clouds,
> We questioned him again and yet again.[22]

Soon, though, they are taken by surprise. Having missed what they'd imagined, they are overwhelmed by wonders they never dreamed of:

> The immeasurable height
> Of woods decaying, never to be decayed,
> The stationary blasts of waterfalls, . . .
> The torrents shooting from the clear blue sky,
> Black drizzling clouds that spake by the way-side . . .
> Tumult and peace, the darkness and the light —
> Were all like workings of one mind, the features
> Of the same face, blossoms upon one tree;
> Characters of the great Apocalypse,
> The types and symbols of Eternity,
> Of first, and last, and midst, and without end.[23]

The eloquence of that last line stands on its own, but Wordsworth hoped readers would be reminded of a passage in *Paradise Lost*: Adam and Eve in a morning hymn to their Creator urging all created beings to extol

Him first, him last, him midst, and without end.[24]

When he equips a passage with a Miltonic marker, Wordsworth is signalling its intended importance. As usual, he's gauged the value of this one correctly. Observe, though, what has happened: elements of the Alpine scenery, once obstructions for miserable travellers, have become "The types and symbols of Eternity." That, and not anything to do with Rome, is one of the supreme feats for which readers of *The Prelude* are grateful.

You may think this marks a termination of the Grand Tour as it was long understood. Rewards from the scenery along the way have replaced those from the destination city. But one further metamorphosis is possible. This is from *Lines Composed a Few Miles Above Tintern Abbey*, which Wordsworth wrote in 1798:

. . . And I have felt
A presence that disturbs me with the joy
Of elevated thoughts; a sense sublime
Of something far more deeply interfused,
Whose dwelling is the light of setting suns,
And the round ocean and the living air,
And the blue sky, and in the mind of man:
A motion and a spirit, that impels
All thinking things, all objects of all thought,
And rolls through all things. . . .[25]

In this single sentence Wordsworth connects us with an Elsewhere unlike those described so far. Even with its setting suns, round ocean, blue sky, and living air, it's not an external landscape. It's not an encounter with Beauty you could experience in a city, in the Roman Forum, in the Sistine Chapel. No, it's an Elsewhere impossible to locate or define in words: it's a "presence," a "sense" of the sublime. This poem, perhaps a thousand words long, has been read and reread now for two centuries.

I'm reminded of a conversation I once had with a man on a train in Taiwan. He informed me that the whole vast oeuvre of the American novelist Henry James was available in Chinese translation. Remembering the intricate Jamesian hierarchies of qualification that inform sentences sometimes half a page long, then reflecting on what I'd been told of the Chinese language with its minimal syntactic mechanisms, I could only ask in astonishment, "What holds it together?" To which his reply was simple: "Reality holds it together."

Henry James and Wordsworth are alike in that respect. A community implies a shared cultural and historical heritage. Another word for that is "reality." It's something each of us experiences, alone.

And so, a final note from William Wordsworth: you'll remember Milton's memory of Galileo, the Tuscan artist with his telescope, viewing the moon

> At Ev'ning from the top of Fesole,
> Or in Valdarno, to descry new Lands,
> Rivers or Mountains in her spotty Globe.

For his parallel in *The Prelude*, Wordsworth invokes a statue

> Of Newton with his prism and silent face,
> The marble index of a mind, forever
> Voyaging through strange seas of thought, alone.[26]

Milton, as we've seen, did visit Galileo; but Sir Isaac Newton (born, as it happens, the year Galileo died) had lived out his long life before Wordsworth's time. So the parallel is abstract: Wordsworth never visited Newton. As a student at Cambridge, he'd visited that statue in the ante-chapel, which is there because Newton was a student and a professor there. Abstract, likewise, is Newton's relation to Galileo: not gazing through an Optic Glass at the moon's spotty globe, but moving through strange intellectual seas in order to describe the laws that govern the moon's motion. We cannot say what Newton was viewing. It's a pure and intricate abstraction, inseparable from the "strange seas of thought." The key word of the passage is its resonant and final "alone."

Aloneness, yet being part of a community. We thrive on Elsewhere Communities, and there are many ways to search for them. The Grand Tour literally took its denizens elsewhere in search of answers to a complex question: who am I? And, an elsewhereness is also what I'm sharing with you right now.

Next, I want to talk about a man who remains, for me, the greatest example of the Elsewhere Community: he's the Elsewhere Community personified. One of the greatest poets of this century, he was the presiding spirit of modernism. Nearly forty years my senior, we met when I was still a graduate student. His name was Ezra Pound and he gave me a piece of advice from which the rest of my life would derive.

II

PORTRAIT OF A MENTOR

WE COMMENCED BY DISCUSSING the Elsewhere Community, "Elsewhere" because you must travel to find it, "Community" because you become a part of it by incorporating it into yourself. In the eighteenth century, as we've seen, an accredited Elsewhere Community for affluent young Englishmen was the city of Rome. That journey was known in its heyday as the Grand Tour.

In 1956, I made a journey like that myself. In the airplane age I could complete it in a few weeks. Its purpose was simple: to meet some half-dozen people, mostly writers, whom I'd decided I simply must visit. And that constellation of visits quickly became an Elsewhere Community of mine, so much so that it's altered everything I've done and written in the four decades since.

That journey was so rich in detail it will need a chapter

to itself. For now, though, I want to tell you about the man who advised me to make it. Through the years, he gave much other valuable advice, to many other people as well as to me. He remains, to my mind, the Elsewhere Community personified. Let me start by telling you how I chanced to meet him.

I was born a Canadian and remain a Canadian citizen, and as to what I'm now doing in the United States, where I've been a green-carded Permanent Resident since 1948, well, the story is intricate and I'll keep it short. In 1946, with a University of Toronto B.A. and M.A. in English, I supposed my academic future was secure. Almost all my instructors had held no degree higher than a British Master of Arts, and so, with a Canadian M.A. of my own, I surely could feel empowered to teach. But that year, thanks to a friend who thought we'd hit it off, I met the universal sage Marshall McLuhan, who convinced me otherwise.

Marshall had just arrived in Toronto and was to be a presence there for the next three decades. His sense of practical reality was then far more acute than mine. He informed me that without a Ph.D. I had no future in this postwar world. So I should obtain one; moreover, I should obtain it at Yale, where his old friend the critic Cleanth Brooks had just arrived. (Marshall did tend to take charge of anyone he was advising.) So in midsummer 1948, he and I set off in my car to visit Cleanth at Yale. And in September, I began my Ph.D. program there. Having since been a director of graduate admissions, I can guess what prodigies of persuasion Cleanth must have performed to get me admitted that late, moreover as an applicant from a foreign country. Hence the green card.

But I've shortened that story by omitting another one. For it was typical of Marshall that we'd driven from Toronto as far as New York before it occurred to him to see whether Cleanth Brooks was in fact in New Haven. A phone call ascertained that he wasn't at present, but would be in three days. So, we had time to put in. And then a chance acquaintance informed us over dinner that it was now possible to visit Ezra Pound. (He'd been imprisoned a year previously in St. Elizabeth's Hospital for the criminally insane, Washington D.C.) Our man, to whom I'm forever indebted, even knew the procedure for setting up a visit. So, en route from New York to New Haven we'd loop through Washington.

On June 4, 1948, Marshall and I pulled in to St. Elizabeth's Hospital. We presented our credentials at the office, saw our names entered in a book labelled "Ezra Pound's Company," then were ushered up two stories to the Chestnut Ward. Pound had recently been promoted from the Dangerously Insane to, so to speak, the Slightly Cracked; that was the news our New York informant was responding to when he'd told us Pound could now be visited. Still, the staircases we climbed were affixed to the outside of the building; inside, floor was sealed from floor. We rang; a guard opened the door; we showed credentials; the door was locked behind us.

Pound, in his new status, had a room of his own, though guests weren't allowed to enter it. Still, he and his wife, Dorothy, an Englishwoman who now used a Washington address, could receive visitors in, well, relative privacy. We all met in an alcove at the intersection of two corridors.

One low armchair for E. P., who had back problems; three more chairs for Dorothy and the two of us. I seem to remember visitors being limited to two. E. P. advised us to pull our chairs in close. He indicated a fellow patient in the corridor, with a carpet-sweeper from which the works had been removed. The man was acting out an obsession about visitors, who tracked in, from the outer world, unspeakable corruption. Pound's old friend and disciple, the poet T. S. Eliot, had recently visited, and owing to a failure to gather the chairs in close, Eliot had spent much of the afternoon with his feet in the air, while the sweeper poked and probed after filth beneath him. That was especially funny if you knew about Eliot's ultra-fastidiousness.

What did Ezra Pound look like? Grey moustache, short grey goatee, grey swept-back hair. His presence could fill a room, or even a makeshift space such as we occupied. Height? Well, I tend to be aware of height, being six-feet-four, myself; but I wasn't aware of his. He was simply very much there. He's routinely described as "tall." That reflects what I call psychic height. (Years later his daughter got me his official height from a passport. five-feet-ten.) Great writers in our time have tended to be tall: T. S. Eliot, five-eleven-and-a-half — a figure I obtained after bumping my head on his six-foot office door. W. B. Yeats and James Joyce, each five-eleven; Sam Beckett, six-two. Save for psychic height, the physical Pound was a midget among giants. But every writer I've just named has mentioned obligations to him. And yet, on the day I met him, June 4, 1948, I barely knew who he was. It was one of the two or three turning points of my life.

I barely knew who he was because my Toronto English curriculum had in effect stopped, as Oxford's then did too, at about 1850, with the death of Wordsworth. Marshall, who'd been at Cambridge instead of Oxford, had subsequently filled me in on lore he'd acquired about the importance of the poet T. S. Eliot, as well as Ezra Pound, author of the 1920 poem "Hugh Selwyn Mauberley." The rest of Pound, it seemed, was sterile: American preoccupation with mere how-to. (How British, such a way of putting things!) But that June day, listening to Pound's talk . . . I learned more than the Cambridge gurus had told Marshall. My subsequent career stems from those two hours. For my major — and mysterious — endowment is a set of antennae. That afternoon they quivered. I knew I was in the presence of the presiding spirit of modernism. I've known ever since how right I was.

Modernism: a simple first-time overview might define it as an extraordinary period in the arts during the first half of the twentieth century. A "return," especially in poetry, to simple words placed in a natural order — no more Tennysonian jewels a-sparkle "on the stretch'd forefinger of all time,"[1] but rather, "Let us go then, you and I . . ."[2] The world the poem inhabits isn't some Camelot or grassy heath; it is, perhaps, today's London. And the hallmarks of today are not shunned; notably, its surrounding technology, subways, cars, telephone, and gramophone. Nothing requires shunning out of being dubbed "unpoetic." And the poem is in no way an "escape" from a dreary world. No, poetry is not an anaesthetic to soothe or lull you into artificial tranquillity.

So, there I was: 1948, in the presence of Ezra Pound, the presiding spirit of modernism. After fifty years, we'll need to fill in some background.

—

Ezra Loomis Pound was born in Hailey, Idaho, in 1885. When I met him he was in his sixty-third year. Early on, he'd seemed destined for a university career. After study, much of it philological, at two universities — the University of Pennsylvania, in Philadelphia, and Hamilton College in upstate New York — Pound taught for a year at a college in Indiana. He then headed for Europe, where he'd been at least twice before. He wanted to advance his education by meeting William Butler Yeats, whom he'd identified — correctly — as the best living poet in the English language, but more on that later.

Pound had lived abroad since his late twenties: in London, then in Paris, then in Rapallo, a small and beautiful Italian town, spectacularly situated on the Gulf of Genoa. As to why he had stayed abroad, instead of returning to a life of college teaching, well, one thing he'd concluded, after his time with Yeats, was that writing poetry was not something to be done on the side. Pound decided he would make writing the focus of his life, and derive the grocery money, as did Yeats, from magazine fees for prose articles on literary, historical, and political subjects that interested him. That would have been impossible in the U.S. of those years, but in London, a sizeable public was buying, for instance, a nicely printed edition of Dante, in pocket-sized volumes with Italian text, notes, and, facing each page, an unpretentious prose version. All of Dante's verse and prose went into a six-volume set, and the price was merely one shilling per volume. Reprints were amazingly frequent; the dates run 1899, 1900, 1901, 1903, 1904, 1908, 1910, 1912 . . . (How large were those printings? Well, in the 1960s, my query got a formulaic answer: such information is "confidential between publisher and author." Let's imagine royalty statements being shoved into Dante's tomb.) And in 1909–10, the London Polytechnic in Regent Street offered a course of lectures largely concerned with Dante and the troubadours. The registrants weren't academic folk as we now understand them; one of them was young Dorothy Shakespear, a designer in watercolours. She subsequently married the lecturer, Ezra Pound. The lectures became the substance of his first prose book, *The Spirit of Romance*. (It was understood that any purchaser would think of "Romance" as the heritage of Rome, not as some trashy novel.)

All this was part of a world not imaginable in the American midwest of those years.

By the end of the First World War, an English periodical called *The New Age* was paying Pound four guineas a month to be both its art critic and its music critic, under pseudonyms. But then, after the war, London no longer seemed alive; life seemed to have moved to Paris, and the Pounds moved to Paris too . . . You see the pattern: Ezra Pound was becoming a bona fide resident of Elsewhere.

All his long life, Pound's theme, his guiding artistic principle, was something he called "Patterned Energy." In his late twenties, he was writing of "our kinship to the vital universe, to the tree and the living rock."[3] Though a human being is "chemically speaking . . . a few buckets of water, tied up in a complicated sort of fig-leaf," still, said Pound, we have our thoughts within us, "as the thought of the tree is in the seed."[4] By 1914, he was using the example of "the whirlpool" or "the vortex" to describe what he meant. Vortex: not the water but a patterned energy made visible by the water.

"Vorticism," as it came to be called, was a way of thinking that reflected not only Pound but the times in which he lived: the age of modernism. In fact, Pound and the writer Wyndham Lewis — a self-proclaimed "vorticist" — even put out a publication called *Blast!*, insisting on vorticist thinking. And in a poem written in 1925, entitled "Among School Children," Yeats would ponder the fact that if a young mother could see her baby as a sixty-year-old, she might well decide the end product wasn't worth the trouble of birth and upbringing. But, said Yeats, it's misleading to think only in terms of an end product. The same unique patterned energy defines the infant and the sexagenarian and every phase in between: "How can we know the dancer from the dance?"

Likewise, Pound thought it pointless to complain about translations where, for example, this English word fails to correspond to that Latin one. For to think so is to think in terms of a classroom crib. For Pound, the translator's real mission was to preserve a "patterned energy" across two languages, not merely to translate the literal meanings of the words. And Pound was a tireless translator. He made the Old English poem "Seafarer," one of the earliest poems written in England, available to modern English writers; likewise the work of the troubadors (the poets of courtly love). They'd written in Old Provençal, and one of them, Arnaut Daniel, was greatly respected by Dante. Then there were the Chinese lyric poets whose work had been available in French translation. Pound got them into English. In fact, he translated so many poems that pedants came to complain, "He can only translate."

But Pound understood the foremost creative minds of his generation and they understood him. In Zurich, for instance, the self-exiled Irishman James Joyce was engaged on the seven-year labour of composing the novel *Ulysses*. He was drawing an eighteen-hour day of Mr. Leopold Bloom, Dublin ad salesman, through a tough pattern defined 2,800 years previously by Homer's *Odyssey*. (*Ulysses* is an odyssey through Dublin that takes place in a single day. In Homer, the odyssey takes ten years and the hero, Odysseus, visits the Kingdom of the Dead. In the corresponding episode, Leopold Bloom attends a funeral in Dublin's Prospect Cemetery.)

Ezra Pound understood and shared James Joyce's vision. They were modernists together. And Pound had a knack for spotting immediate needs. What Joyce needed most was an English-language advocate, someone to make the case for his importance. In article after article, Pound tirelessly filled the role. Conversely, in 1922, when he at last read *Ulysses* as a whole — for years he'd been seeing it in excerpts as they were completed — Pound came to a clear understanding of what he was attempting in his own magnum opus, *The Cantos*: it would begin where Dante left off, surveying cultural landmarks and turning points since the Renaissance. And the West's discovery of China would feature prominently. That was about as much of a plan as he had. His way was always to move from large themes to smaller details.

In eighteenth-century England we find poets helping one another with revisions; marking lines for revision, drafting replacements. As Samuel Johnson remarked, the difficulty was not to make verses, but to know when you had made good ones. Hence the advantage of help. During the next century's Romantic revolution, such help became impossible, what got on paper having become a deposit left by an irreproducible bout of inspiration, something another hand could only adulterate. But in twentieth-century modernism, finding the language for what was to be said had once again become an occupation colleagues could share. The most influential poem of the first half of the century was, perhaps, T. S. Eliot's 1922 *The Waste Land*. Five decades later, the publication of the working drafts would reveal *The Waste Land* to have been, in many respects, a collaboration.

When it reached its final form and acquired its final title, Eliot dedicated the poem "To Ezra Pound, il miglior fabbro." He was quoting what Dante had written six centuries earlier about Arnaut Daniel, the troubador poet Dante had admired. In *The Divine Comedy*, Dante calls Daniel "il miglior fabbro del parlar materna," the better craftsman in the mother tongue. In his dedication, Eliot was overtly acknowledging the fact that he and Pound both approached English from an American angle. He was also tacitly indicating that Pound had contributed to the actual text of *The Waste Land* itself. There'd long been rumours to that effect, and in the 1950s, when I asked him about it, Pound phrased his response carefully: "*The Waste Land* was laid before me as a series of poems," he said. "I advised him on what to leave out."

When Eliot's widow published the surviving drafts in 1973, I learned that Pound had done much more than that. He'd restructured stretches of over-regular meter, and had so fussed at some passages that Eliot ended up rewriting them entirely. Indeed, Eliot achieved some of his finest heights in the process of bringing some limpness or other up from blather. What the two of them were working on finally shrank to less than half its original length. No longer a series of poems, it became nineteen double-spaced typed pages, entitled *The Waste Land*, a single work in five parts which Pound, on receiving the typescript, called "let us say the longest poem in the English langwidge." Pound had also impressed on the poem the example of Yeats, for whom Eliot at that time had small regard. Yeats had also made long poems out of sequences of short ones. And in 1922, Pound himself was starting to follow that model in his own life-long work: a sequence of 117 poems he called *The Cantos*. If Eliot had put together *The Waste Land* without, as one reviewer complained, knowing "what he wanted to say," well, so much the better. A poet who knows what it is he wants to say may be sure it's been said already.

Pound's ability to help his friends seems to have somewhat outpaced his own development. Possibly, though, it was in helping them that he learned of his own poetic destiny.

Back in 1911, on a visit to Paris, he'd alighted from the Paris underground railroad — the Metro — where, he recalled, he "saw suddenly a beautiful face, and then another and another . . . and I tried all that day to find words for what they had meant to me."[5] He'd first thought of some wholly abstract vision of colours: splotches on darkness, like one of Kandinsky's canvasses. Then he wrote, and destroyed, a thirty-line poem; later, a shorter one was destroyed too. By 1913, he'd arrived at a two-line poem which needs every one of its twenty words, including the six words of its title:

IN A STATION OF THE METRO
The apparition of these faces in the crowd;
Petals on a wet, black bough.[6]

"Petals on a wet, black bough": that's normal spoken language. No need for Tennysonian "Jewels five words long"; no "Bold Sir Bedivere uplifted him,"[7] meaning simply that he was carried because he couldn't walk and not "uplifted" in any evangelical sense . . . Lord, what a mess the diction of poetry had become. Then came Elsewhere.

Pound's "In a Station of the Metro" is in every sense an Elsewhere poem. He took Elsewhere eyes to Paris. He adapted an Elsewhere poetic form — the haiku — from

Japan. He arrived at two lines inseparable from their title, the whole phenomenon free of emotional slither.

—⁂—

Back to the summer of 1948. I may not have known much then about Ezra Pound the poet, but I did know something about Ezra Pound the American: specifically, what he was doing in a hospital for the criminally insane. And as the years went on, I found out even more about that.

Like some other non-Italian intellectuals — Winston Churchill, for one — Pound had become, in the 1920s, an avid Mussolini-watcher. About one thing he was certainly right: Mussolini, a well-read man who spoke several languages, was by no means to be confused with the hysterical Hitler.

By early 1941, living in Italy, and driven both by fervour and dire financial need (his book royalties from abroad having all been cut off), Pound was spending seven to ten days a month in Rome, recording broadcasts for transmission to America. By mid-1943, the U.S. government had indicted him for treason. His response reads in part, "I have not spoken with regard to this war, but in protest against a system which creates one war after another, in series and in system. I have not spoken to the troops, and have not suggested that the troops should mutiny or revolt."[8] On May 3, 1945, four days before the formal end of the European war, Pound was taken into American custody.

The time he spent in the detention training centre near Pisa — part of it in a cage under a twenty-four-hour guard with night-long searchlights — may well have damaged his sanity. Brought back to Washington the following spring, he was met by his long-time publisher James Laughlin, who once told me that he seemed "confused." Next, following legal advice, he pleaded not guilty by reason of insanity, and was confined in a hospital for the criminally insane, which was where Marshall McLuhan and I went to see him.

Ezra Pound was the first man I'd ever met who always spoke in complete sentences. His first utterance that afternoon was a subordinate clause: "Since you are younger and more vigorous than I, perhaps you will not mind if I sit here."

Having learned that Marshall was a college teacher, and I an aspiring one, Pound spoke about the need for attention to the curriculum. Which writers should we be regarding as important? Well, for instance, the man of letters Ford Madox Ford. That especially piqued my interest because, back when I was sixteen, a librarian in Peterborough, Ontario, had pushed in my direction a book by Ford called *The March of Literature*. Amid the reminiscences it offered were some about a poet named Ezra Pound: the first time I'd looked at that name. And here, to complete a circle, was Pound, the first man from whom I'd ever heard mention of Ford Madox Ford. (On the drive home, Marshall, then still besotted by Cambridge orthodoxy, would remark of Ford that he was "Oh, pretty feeble." He isn't. Start with his 1915 novel, *The Good Soldier*. Originally called *The Saddest Story*, it's one of the most astonishingly constructed novels ever written. Or start with one Pound recommended, *A Call*: "That thing has structure," he said admiringly. Yet what earns the structure is the transparent diction, which, said Pound, "just lay so natural on the page you didn't notice it." Pound said he once tried to make a note of something of Ford's, but found he couldn't reduce it to fewer words than Ford had used.)

I'd brought with me a copy of *Personae*, Pound's collected shorter poems, hoping he'd inscribe it, which he graciously did. What Marshall brought for inscription was a copy of the *Pisan Cantos*, which had just come out, though to little notice, the writer being "obscure." After we got back, though, a fuss about it would reach an unheard-of crescendo. But the fuss wasn't about poetry; it was about the book being named for what was called the Bollingen Prize, an award then given by the Library of Congress and now largely forgotten.

There'd been an earlier fuss, in 1946, when Random House proposed to exclude Pound altogether from a new edition of their *Anthology of Famous English and American Poetry*, which previously had offered twelve Pound selections. "We're not going to publish any fascist," said their spokesman. "In fact, we don't think that Ezra Pound is good enough, or important enough, to include."[9] They later admitted receiving 142 letters opposing the exclusion, versus 140 approving. The poems were included.

But the 1948 Bollingen fuss was much noisier. Though the jurors stood their ground and the *Pisan Cantos* got selected, the *Saturday Review of Literature* (a then influential weekly, now defunct) published tirade after tirade. And a Joint Committee of the United States House and Senate ruled that the Library of Congress must abstain in the future from giving any prizes or awards whatsoever. Even Radio Moscow put in a word: "One is prompted to ask how poetry in America if even the insane and verified ravings of a confessed madman could win a literary prize?"[10]

Browsers who found the *Cantos* puzzling did have a point. One day, I was driving Marshall and his mother somewhere. She found a copy of the *Pisan Cantos* in the car. "Marshall!" she said sharply. "Marshall! What does all this mean?" Marshall was suave. "Well mother, you have to understand that in the poetry you're used to, things happen one after another. But in that kind of poetry, everything happens at once."

The Bollingen fuss appalled me. What was chiefly appalling was that the United States literati, including the distinguished jurors who'd awarded the prize, were all busy defending the integrity of the awards process. No one at all was defending Pound. Supposing I had nothing to lose, and in fact too naive to realize I was risking my entire future, I decided that if no one would speak up for him, I would.

In the summer of 1948, on a picnic table overlooking Lake Chemong near Peterborough, on a little borrowed Corona portable typewriter that lacked a right-hand margin stop, I put in six-hour workdays, mid-July through August. I fetched books from the University of Toronto library ninety miles away — books I needed, because, as it turned out, the best guide to Pound's poetry was his prose, a fact that seemed not to have been noticed before. The result was the 308 typed pages of *The Poetry of Ezra Pound*, published in 1951 by Pound's British publisher and also his

American one. It did make a difference, if only by helping usher Pound onto the curriculum. When there's a "book about," all concerned feel much more secure. And Pound wrote me, making a couple of brief corrections, then offering congratulations on so many pages with "no more than that to notate."

—

After the summer we first met, Pound and I stayed in touch. Once settled that fall in New Haven, I was to return to Washington again and again and remained in touch with Pound after I'd moved in 1950, with my new degree, to my first job: University of California, Santa Barbara. (I remained in the U.S. because, back then, no Canadian university was interested in what I could teach, which was English literature later than their 1850-ish cutoff date.) Face to face, by letters, and by printed pages, Pound continued in his role as mentor.

"HK not leaving blanks for what he doesn't know," was his note on a draft of mine. And here's the kind of letter I'd get from him:

> Might be useful if K/ did article on what he has seen
> since his bk/ on EZ. Time to fight scatter/ and possibly
> distinguish NECESSARY education from books that a stu-
> dent with any talent for reading wd read on his own for
> enjoyment.

The "NECESSARY" education consisted of four names he abbreviated: the Confucian classics, Dante's *Divine*

Comedy, Sir William Blackstone's *Commentaries on the Laws of England*, and the close observations of the scientist Alexander Agassiz. They are all distinguished by relevance of content and exactness of phrasing. The presence of Confucius, Blackstone, and Agassiz in that list led him to his next sentence: "A culture is NOT affair of writers alone." For Pound, that was a fact writers always needed to be reminded of.

The things that would matter, Pound tended to compress into single sentences. How to start a piece of writing? "Find out where the subject begins." To end it? "Introduce new material near the end." That arose from a question about how *The Cantos* was progressing. He'd stated that there was material still to be introduced and he'd stop when that process had ended. The composition class formula, "Tell 'em what you're going to tell 'em, tell 'em, tell 'em what you told 'em," was something he scorned. (I've used the procedures he advocated ever since; they always work.)

Eccentric though he could seem in the 1940s, Pound was following a tradition then more than a century old, when Americans wanted to revisit European culture, but at the same time protect an American identity they valued. For instance, though he lived abroad for much of his life, the American novelist Henry James was at pains never to de-Americanize his language. "That was the real way to work things out"[11]: no Briton would have published such a sentence; its shading of "real," for one thing, is unknown to the ultra-British *Oxford English Dictionary*. T. S. Eliot, by contrast, achieved a neutral idiom: mid-Atlantic, as it were.

Educated American, yes; or, yes, educated British. As for Ezra Pound, the *OED*, second edition, cites the Pound of 1909 as the documentable first to use the word persona (that's Latin for a player's mask) to designate the role the writer plays in the writing. And throughout his long life, Pound's idiom of the moment, written or spoken, was a form of role-playing.

There's a tradition behind that. The easiest mask to which the printed page, or the typewriter, affords a writer access is achieved by tinkering with spelling. Nineteenth-century American humorists — Joel Chandler Harris, Artemus Ward, Mark Twain — had long elevated phonetic spelling into a style. They were signalling their detachment from the schoolmarm culture they mocked by recording their characters' idiom rather than the classroom's. That was an early symptom, their perception that while an education was indispensable, it had better not be allowed to affect you too much. And so Pound, despite years spent in pursuit of higher education,would maintain their tradition by reverting, in most of his thousands of typewritten letters, to the crackerbarrel sage who spelled everything just as it sounded.

Here's a wonderful example from a letter he wrote me in the late 1940s — handwritten, not typewritten, but jam-packed with his characteristic spelling (or rather, mis-spelling):

> Dear HK:
> Nacherly you can't egg-speck a prefessor to read fer to learn wot he don't know . . .

I've forgotten the context, but you get the drift. On the other hand, for two decades from the day I met him, I was continually impressed by the formality of his spoken syntax.

It's instructive to watch the manipulation of roles in the forty-year magnum opus Pound called simply *The Cantos*. As the first canto opens he's a ninth-century Anglo-Saxon bard:

> We set up mast and sail on that swart ship,
> Bore sheep aboard her, and our bodies also
> Heavy with weeping, and winds from sternward
> Bore us out onward with bellying canvas . . .[12]

As the same canto ends, two pages later, he's a scholar leading classroom students through the words of a Renaissance Latin text:

> Venerandam,
> In the Cretan's phrase, with the golden crown,
> Aphrodite,
> . . . oricalchi, with golden
> Girdles and breast bands, thou with dark eyelids . . .[13]

Always, he's someone else, who is frequently some fragment of himself — a fifteenth-century Italian chronicler; an American moved to Italy; a disciple of Chinese sages. Even when (just once) he's "E. P.," or (three times) the "scriptor cantilenae," writer of *Cantos*, he's assuming but one more role among many. It's important also to grasp that for Pound a role was not an assumed costume of unreality. No, a Poundian role was an aspect of reality, the aspect that at this moment, for complex reasons, comes uppermost.

Even more than Poet, American was a role — a role he regarded as crucial despite the fact that he might have avoided the endless problems of his late life (the indictment, the imprisonment) had he simply adopted Italian citizenship, say around 1930. But no, to have inherited by birthright and education the intellectual and social clarities of Thomas Jefferson and John Adams, that heritage couldn't be discarded. It was always central to his sense of his own identity. It was what he thought licensed him to speak, over Rome Radio, as an American, to Americans he'd never seen and would never see, apprising them of what he thought was really going forward in Mussolini's Rome that American papers were staying mum about. Serious scholarship has now been devoted to the entanglements of those Roman years. I can recommend Tim Redman's book, *Ezra Pound and Italian Fascism*. Myself, I'll stick with what I saw and heard. And I never heard him make either a political statement or a racist one.

Then there was Pound's role as mentor. Where did it come from? He'd learned it from his own mentor, the Irish poet William Butler Yeats, whose role in Pound's development cannot be overestimated.

Pound especially admired Yeats's ability to fit a complex sentence, exactly and repeatedly, into a stanza of any

length. Other nineteenth-century poets in English tended
to pay little heed to syntactic boundaries. If we identify a
sentence as the verbiage that separates full-stops, then
Tennysonian sentences can readily be found that meander
for twenty-odd lines. But listen to Yeats, who pretends to be
a fisherman uttering malediction on an unco-operative fish,
though he'll be letting us guess that the fish was human:

THE FISH

Although you hide in the ebb and flow
Of the pale tide when the moon has set,
The people of coming days will know
About the casting out of my net,
And how you have leaped times out of mind
Over the little silver cords,
And think that you were hard and unkind,
And blame you with many bitter words.[14]

— sixty words, all but seven of them monosyllabic; eight
rhymed lines, yet just one sentence, beginning with an
"Although" clause that introduces a formally structured
three-part prediction.

Centuries ago, an Irish bard had two main duties: to
praise the king's friends, to curse the king's enemies. It
was understood that the bard's curses, being knowingly
constructed, were efficacious, unlike modern ones which
merely relieve the curser's feelings. And in exemplifying a
principal Irish bardic form, "The Fish" is as cool a curse as
ever a bard contrived. The voice is never raised, while in
the guise of a fish, what's being cursed is (surely!) some

maddeningly unresponsive woman. Yeats contrived that small wonder as early as 1898; he was thirty-three.

In September 1908, Ezra Pound, M.A., age nigh twenty-three, arrived in London intent on meeting Yeats, who was forty-three. Yeats, as so often, wasn't there. They met eventually in April 1909. Yeats had just come back from the funeral of J. M. Synge, the great playwright who wrote *The Playboy of the Western World*. Synge had lived to write only six plays. (Reflect that Shakespeare's sixth play was merely *Titus Andronicus*.) And so, with no playwright of Synge's stature in sight, no prose writer worth attention (Joyce had not yet published a book), and no notable Irish poet save himself, Yeats was close to despair about Ireland's literary future.

As it happened, the Yeats-Pound timing could not have been better. The incantatory Yeats, by whom Pound had long been enchanted, was becoming a figure of history. That fact owes something to the Romantic postulate that lyric poetry is something men write when they're young and had best give up by the time they're forty. Witness Wordsworth, who'd lived, it was thought, far too long. Accordingly, Yeats's *Collected Works*, eight volumes of verse and prose, had appeared in 1908 like the deposit of debris that follows a huge glacier. Yeats was then forty-three. Thereafter, he spent more than half his life, and wrote more than three-quarters of his poetry, in the twentieth century, never succumbing to the Wordsworthian slump.

The price of such poetic longevity was a long and very deliberate self-remaking. When he and Pound met, the off-hand lyricism of "I made it out of a mouthful of air"[15]

(Yeats in 1899) was in the course of being supplanted by the bitter chill of the 1904 poem "Adam's Curse," which is candid about how poetry is made:

> . . . Better go down upon your marrow-bones
> And scrub a kitchen pavement, or break stones
> Like an old pauper, in all kinds of weather;
> For to articulate sweet sounds together
> Is to work harder than all these, and yet
> Be thought an idler by the noisy set
> Of bankers, schoolmasters, and clergymen
> The martyrs call the world.[16]

That, by the way, was only one sentence. And so, to the great profit of twentieth-century poetry in English, Pound was to spend three winters (1913–16) in Sussex, ostensibly as Yeats's "secretary," while they hammered out the Irish and the Anglo-American versions of English-language modernism.

So in those years, Yeats was Pound's mentor, and Pound learned exactly what he needed to be taught: the close relationship of poetry and common speech. In this way, as memorable an Elsewhere Community was formed as this century has seen. For it had two members, each one teaching the other. Yeats valued all his life the reinforcement his newly developing manner received from Pound. ("Discuss a poem with him, and all comes clear."[17]) And the value of normal, speakable words that offered a grip on normal realities was what Pound in turn would be teaching innumerable acolytes.

Back in the U.S. they still thought otherwise. The first number of Harriet Monroe's Chicago magazine, *Poetry* (September 1912), opened with a sonnet called "Poetry" by someone called A. D. Ficke. Its sestet began,

> It is a refuge from the stormy days,
> Breathing the peace of a remoter world
> Where beauty, like the musking dusk of even,
> Enfolds the spirit in its silver haze. . . .

Whereas on T. S. Eliot's "The Love Song of J. Alfred Prufrock," which Pound relayed to her in 1914, Miss Monroe was to sit, undecided, for months. "A patient etherized upon a table." Poetry, indeed! Harriet seemed unresponsive, utterly, to the wistful eloquence of passages such as:

> And I have known the arms already, known them all,
> Arms that are braceleted and white and bare
> (But in the lamplight, downed with light brown hair!)
> Is it perfume from a dress
> That makes me so digress?
> Arms that lie along a table, or wrap about a shawl. . . .[18]

She finally published it, with the author's name misspelled, only after Pound had been admonishing her for months: "DO get on with that Eliot!"

Mentoring: that became second nature to Pound.

When James Laughlin, an heir to the Jones and Laughlin steel fortune, graduated from Harvard in the mid-1930s, his next move was to head for Italy and meet a man he'd been corresponding with. He'd call that enrolling in "the EZ-University," as it were, for graduate work. Pound persuaded him that his verse, though meritorious, had a thinner future to offer a literate man with some money, such as Laughlin, than did founding a small avant-garde publishing house — something the U.S. very badly needed. Major houses published poets as window-dressing, and were apt to quickly cancel what didn't sell. Laughlin's response was to found and manage New Directions, American publisher for, notably, Ezra Pound and William Carlos Williams. Williams, in particular, had never before had a real publisher, just fly-by-nights. Laughlin understood the need to keep all their works in print until sales started to pick up, which might take decades. (And it did take decades, but it happened.) Laughlin went on writing his own poems, but he let other small houses publish them.

All manner of people would profit from the EZ-University. "What I owe Ezra!" a Canadian novelist named John Reid once wrote to me. For himself, John had trouble getting published anywhere at all; but he helped me, at any rate, reading my typescripts with a Poundian eye. And he felt at peace with his own unpublished work.

One day, towards the middle of the 1950s, during one of my visits to St. Elizabeth's Hospital, Ezra Pound told me, in a context I completely forget,

> You have an ob-li-ga-tion
> to visit
> the great men of your own time.

I foreground that as the single most pregnant sentence I've ever heard uttered. I had no idea then that what he was proposing amounted to a mid-twentieth-century Grand Tour. Two further themes were implied: (1) that it was up to me to make my own Greatness list; (2) that if he could help with any people I listed, as with addresses or introductions, he would gladly oblige. (As it happened, the sole address he offered that I didn't use was Hemingway's. I simply couldn't manage the cost of a round trip between California and Cuba.)

So, early in November 1956, I was headed (for my first time) to Europe, on a four-engine Lockheed Constellation that could grind its propellers from Newfoundland to Shannon, Ireland, before refuelling. We'll be talking about that journey. For now, a last look at Pound:

By and large, he'd known back in the 19-teens that his future was in Europe, the coming horrors of which — 1914–18 and 1939–45 — no one, he least of all, foresaw. One thing that had aided his decision to stay in Europe (London, Paris, Rapallo) once the first of those wars had ended was his native country's Prohibition Amendment; not that he was a drinker, for he wasn't. But that a people at peace could be patient with a government that meddled to that extent! . . . So his Elsewhere Community turned out to be Europe — some would say Darkest Europe — during decades when he was persuading himself that his prime allegiance was to American liberty.

In late years, after they'd charitably discharged him from St. Elizabeth's Hospital (the excuse was that he was "incurably insane") he lived for a while with his daughter

Mary in her castle in the Tirolean Alps. On the wall of his room hung a large American flag. He died in Venice in 1972; back in his Tirolean room, the flag hangs yet.

My wife and I last saw Pound in Venice, in 1966. He was almost wholly silent. "You ordered that for me?" His companion, Olga Rudge, responded, "Yes, Ezra. Eat it." And he did. The mentor, you might say, mentored? That was a relationship he'd always understood.

III

AND I SEE FOR MYSELF

BEHOLD ME, THEN, IN 1956, embarked on a re-enactment of the classic Grand Tour to where the Great resided. My list of whom I'd visit began with those still alive from the generation that had made the lasting literature of our time. W. B. Yeats and James Joyce were dead. T. S. Eliot, though, was still active in London, and so was his and Pound's old sparring partner, Wyndham Lewis. In America resided William Carlos Williams and Marianne Moore, two poets of international visibility.

What was common to these writers — notably a commitment to plain modern language and to assimilating today's urban environment — has since come to be called modernism, though by normal definitions of movements, which posit an organizer and a manifesto, modernism was atypical. Two sorts of writers dominated it: Irishmen, often self-exiled, and Americans who lived abroad. (Williams was defiant in not living abroad, though he'd spent many months in Europe and was fluent in two languages besides English. But in so defining himself he was modernist too.) And the archetypal American Writer Abroad was Henry James, who lived from 1843 clear until 1916, which was long enough for Ezra Pound to have known him.

I once heard Ezra Pound imitate Henry James's speech at some length, and it sounded exactly as intricate as James's writing. One afternoon in the late 1950s, hunching his shoulders forward, hands clasped between his knees, Pound became for some ninety seconds Henry James, eyes fixed on a point in space some yards past a ghostly auditor. He was imitating what had mesmerized him at age twenty-six: James piling up a long sentence in elaborate phrase after phrase, like a man slowly cranking up a pile driver, with many pauses, labourings, diversions, and much mopping of the brow, until suddenly a huge weight fell with a SPLAT.

Here's a sentence James published in 1888. It addresses the way art lives, yet somehow splats down with the word "dullness":

Art lives upon discussion, upon experiment, upon curiosity, upon variety of attempt, upon the exchange of views and the comparison of standpoints; and there is a presumption that those times when no one has anything particular to say about it, and has no reason to give for practice or preference, though they may be times of honor, are not times of development — are times, possibly even, a little of dullness.[1]

James had been abroad as an infant. At age twelve he went abroad a second time, so he and his brother could, as their father said, "absorb French and German and get a better sensuous education" than they'd likely get in New York, where they were also acquiring "shocking bad manners from the street."[2] Henry James, fastidious until the end of his life, pretty much settled in Europe in about 1882 at age thirty-nine. In 1897, he moved to Lamb House, Rye, East Sussex. If you visit the house today, you'll notice the width of the front door and doorstep. You can easily imagine his dog, Maximilian, winding and rewinding a leash round his master's ankles while the great voice lifts itself in yet one more endless sentence.

In 1904–05, he'd essay a last look at America, "a society trying to build itself, with every elaboration, into some coherent sense of itself, and literally putting forth interrogative feelers, as it goes, into the ambient air."[3] That need to get back to the Europe their ancestors had found good reason to leave was always present in Henry James, and later in Ezra Pound and T. S. Eliot.

So, early in November 1956, I was headed for my first time towards Europe, on a Lockheed Constellation. (A coupon entitled you to a certificate stating that you had, indeed, crossed the Atlantic — and by air!) After landing in Shannon, it was on to Dublin, where that generous man, the late poet-critic Donald Davie, took me to meet Georgie Yeats, the widow of W. B. Yeats.

Mrs. Yeats received us in her drawing room. It was lined with original engravings of the Book of Job, by William Blake, whom her husband had helped discover. In those pre-Xerox days, Mrs. Yeats kept on hand a few manuscript pages of her husband's writing, encased in plastic, for sharing with visitors. The one that detained me the longest (if I'm not misremembering) was a pencil draft of the poem "Sailing to Byzantium." As I hesitated, mumbling over its third or fourth word, she came to my rescue with "Oh, he never could spell!" It's important to record that she spoke those words not dismissively but with affection.

Speaking of Elsewhere Communities, Georgie Yeats, a Brit, had by then lived in Ireland some forty years, and W. B., Dublin-born but long transplanted to a different world — the northeast Irish coast — had died where he'd spent much of his last years, in southern France, although he was much later buried in Ireland. It's hard to call to mind a major figure of the Irish Revival who didn't die abroad. Joyce died in Zurich, Sean O'Casey in the south of England, even Oliver Gogarty — to whom Joyce alludes in the very first words of *Ulysses* as "Stately, plump Buck Mulligan" — a man so contrary he had even, he would boast, let loose some snakes in Ireland to counter St. Patrick's gesture in abolishing them; even he complied with a convention he'd never have recognized by dying in New York.

It was Georgie Yeats, whose spells of automatic writing, begun shortly after their 1917 marriage, had fuelled Yeats's last mystical phase. The spirits, with whom meditation put her in touch, had dictated the substance of what became his strange book, called *A Vision* — a work that professed to be everyone's horoscope, as well as a grand outline of human history running, as it did, through 2,000-year phases, and as a bonus offering, so Yeats said, "metaphors for poetry." Yet how normal, in 1956, the amanuensis of the spirits seemed! That was an enlightenment.

———

England next; and, on Davie's recommendation, the British bard Charles Tomlinson, then residing at the unforgettable address The Old Rectory, Hinton Blewett, Temple Cloud, Glos. Charles and his wife, Brenda, showed me Bath Cathedral; Charles read me his poems, gave me one of his paintings, and sold me another. We've been fast friends ever since.

It is unusual to meet a poet on a recommendation, and only after to become acquainted with his work. Yet the poet's presence introduced the work fittingly, for Tomlinson said things in a very straightforward way — one that we've learned to call "modernist."

"Those midland '*a*'s' once cost me a job,"[4] said Tomlinson in one of his poems. That's so; despite his Cambridge degree, there were jobs he couldn't aspire to, on account of an accent that I, not being English, was at a loss to detect. ("The Englishman," Wyndham Lewis wrote long ago, "is branded on the tongue at birth."[5]) The University of Bristol, to its credit, added Charles Tomlinson to its staff.

Here's another example of Tomlinson's work: an early poem, called simply, "Paring the Apple."

There are portraits and still-lives.

And there is paring the apple.

And then? Paring it slowly,
From under cool-yellow
Cold-white emerging. And . . . ?

The spring of concentric peel
Unwinding off white,
The blade hidden, dividing.

There are portraits and still-lives
And the first, because "human"
Does not excel the second, and
Neither is less weighted
With a human gesture, than paring the apple
With a human stillness.

The cool blade
Severs between coolness, apple-rind
Compelling a recognition.[6]

You'll have noticed the clear, cool statement, not an obscure
word. Evident too is the stated affinity with visual art. The
party line used to be that poetry's affinities were with music.
(And when will England again know who its poets are?)

And in London . . . "When a man is tired of London,"
Samuel Johnson remarked more than two hundred years
ago, "he is tired of life."[7] Yes, there was much to see. London

also still contained two eminent veterans of modernism's originating days. T. S. Eliot, you're thinking; yes. But don't forget Wyndham Lewis. My pattern became this: each evening, on finishing my day's explorations, I'd revert for a couple of hours to the Notting Hill Gate flat where Lewis, by then totally blind, would have finished his own daily round. At one time, Lewis had been a distinguished painter. And back on the eve of World War One, he'd founded the periodical *Blast!*, which the war cut off after two issues. His major collaborator had been Ezra Pound, who'd coined for Lewis's use the word "Vorticism": all creativity defining a "Vortex of Energy." You can see why I needed to meet him.

In his blind state, Lewis's creativity now consisted mainly of writing. On the right-hand arm of his blue armchair, there sat a pad; in his right hand, a pen. (I presented him with an American ballpoint, the service life of which notably exceeded that of its then British rivals. That was important because a blind man wouldn't know if his ballpoint quit.) Using three fingers of his left hand, after each written line he would measure down the page a width great enough to keep lines from intersecting. That permitted a five-line page, which, completed, would be torn from the pad and dropped on the floor for Froanna (Mrs. Lewis) to retrieve and type. She'd later read the typescript back to him, for corrections. In that way, the two of them had completed, since his blindness, seven published books. (His publisher, Methuen, deserved great credit for supporting a blind author who had never been fashionable.)

Upstairs, in the studio where he'd painted his post-

Vorticist wonders, dust gathered on scattered drawings. When his blindness became final (due to an inoperable tumour), he'd informed readers of *The Listener* that his service as their art critic must end, since "I can no longer see a picture."[8] He might have added, but didn't, that he was no more handicapped than other London art critics one might think of. "Pushed into an unlighted room," wrote Lewis, "the door banged and locked for ever, I shall have to light a lamp of aggressive voltage to keep at bay the night."[9] To which add one other imperishable phrase from Lewis: "Milton had his daughters, I have my dictaphone."

But alas, imperishable phrases may see realities mutate. The dictaphone was superseded by Lewis's need to work hands-on: to actually hold the pen in his own hand.

One memorable day was November 18, 1956: Wyndham Lewis's seventy-fourth (and last) birthday. That was when I learned about one aspect of his disability: since he was unable to see where people were standing, he could no longer gauge the appropriate volume for his voice. (Geoffrey Bridson of the BBC would later tell me of a meal at Scott's Oyster House, where Lewis spoke of a Sir —— who'd have paid him a large sum to marry A—— B——. "In a voice you could have heard as far as Picadilly Circus," Bridson said Lewis had shouted, "'I couldn't stand the thought of waking up with that face beside me on the bed.'") And at the birthday dinner, asked if he'd have more of something, he shouted, "NO!!!!," whereupon Froanna memorably said, "You mustn't mind Wyndham shouting. It's just . . . high spirits!" That indefatigable energy! And her devotion! I'd never seen the like.

Memorable too was the day, soon after, when I finally met T. S. Eliot. Ezra Pound had named Eliot the Possum, mindful, he once told me, of Brer Possum in the Uncle Remus stories: "Ol' Possum, he jest lie low an' say nuffin." Well, no one actually met T. S. Eliot: one met a role, of which the Possum had a variety, as for instance the Archdeacon, the Publisher, the American in Europe. But one never met the Poet.

Eliot was born in St. Louis, where his grandfather had founded Washington University. He was educated at Harvard, where his grandfather's third cousin once removed had been president for forty years and had edited a five-foot shelf of Classics, once sold door to door. Eliot had appropriately foreseen a Harvard chair, and had gone to Germany for graduate work — Germany having been where advanced study, in those days, was concentrated. Arriving in the summer of 1914, he'd been engulfed by war, was shipped to England in an exchange of aliens, married an Englishwoman, and stayed there. After time spent clerking in a bank, he'd found work at a publishing house, Faber & Gwyer, later Faber & Faber, of which he'd risen to the status of director. Their letterhead had at one time noted next to his name, "American Origin." In that world, roles certainly mattered.

Faber had been the British publisher of a book of mine, *The Poetry of Ezra Pound*, so to what Eliotic role was I entitled? He decided on the London Clubman. Thus we met at his high-toned London club, the Garrick. It was soon evident that the Possum was casting me as Huck Finn.

Clubman Eliot first interpreted the menu. "Now there is jugged hare. That is a very English dish. Do you want to be English? Or do you want to be . . . safe?" And later: "Now. Will you have a sweet? Or . . . cheese?" The answer of choice was so evidently "cheese" that I leaped to specify it, perhaps a little too rapidly. "Are you sure? You can have ice cream, you know." At the Garrick! I remained firm about cheese. "Very well," said Eliot. "I fancy a fine Stilton." And as the waiter went for it, "Never commit yourself to a cheese without having first examined it." What was placed in front of the Great Critic was accordingly Examined. He tapped the circumference of the cheese with his knife-blade, head cocked in a listening posture. Its top being hollowed out like a lunar crater, he next tapped the crater's inner wall. Last, his knife dug amid fragments contained in the crater. And the verdict: "Rather past its prime. I am afraid I cannot recommend it."

The Stilton vanished, to be replaced by a cheese-board, each denizen of which was tapped, prodded, sounded. One he segregated: "A rather fine Red Cheshire, which you might enjoy." The intonation on "you" did not invite assessment. He next devoted his attention to a toadstool-yellow specimen, tapped, poked, prodded, scraped. "What is that?" Ignorance of the waiter. "Could we find out?" Waiter vanishes. Two substitutes appear. Eliot points. They shrug. "Aha! An anonymous cheese!" Having sampled a slice, he transferred it to his plate, and proceeded without further ceremony to consume to the last crumb the entire anonymous cheese.

That evening Wyndham Lewis heard the story. "Oh,

never mind him," said Lewis. "He's like that with everybody. But he doesn't come *in here* disguised as Westminster
Abbey." Nine years later, both the story and the story of
Lewis hearing the story were narrated, in Venice, to the
octogenarian Ezra Pound, then almost totally engulfed in
the deliberate silence of his final years. And what Pound
finally responded to was Lewis's response, at which the
supreme Old Man of Modern Letters threw back his head
to refresh the Italian air with peals of hearty laughter.

The variety of Eliot's roles invites study. If that day at the
Garrick he came on as more British than the British
(a remarkable stretch), he'd been at other times more
American than the Americans. One year Faber & Faber
had the maladresse to schedule a directors' meeting for the
fourth of July. He rigged the meeting room with a rope
which ran from his chair to a leg of the managing director's
chair, then back to a metal waste-basket under the table
near him. The basket was filled with firecrackers in deadly
connection. At a suitable moment, Eliot lit the crackers,
then pulled on the rope, so it was beneath the director's
chair that everything exploded, rat-a-tat-tat BOOM. One up
for America!

At the Garrick, during a lull in the conversation, I asked
Eliot whether he had any advice on the procurement of
a suit. I had a ready-made in mind, but his response was
to offer the name of his tailor: Mr. Cyril Langley, on
Albemarle Street. ("That's an expensive street," was the
comment of Wyndham Lewis.) Since Eliot tended to figure

on lists of well-dressed men, I decided that a visit to his tailor might be interesting.

A little rotund man with a measuring tape draped around his neck answered the door. I inquired about the possibility of having a suit made for export.

"Yes, Sir. And, ah, have you been recommended, Sir?"

I was able to respond, "Why, yes, Mr. T. S. Eliot gave me your name."

"Ah, Mr. Eliot! And what did you say your name was, Sir?"

After a choice of fabric, and much measuring, I returned a day or two later for a ritual known as The Fitting. The suit had been cut and basted together, and was now hung on me while Mr. Langley cluck-clucked and retouched its fit with marking chalk and pins. At one point he removed all the pins from his mouth to venture on something oracular.

"Remarkable man, Mr. Eliot."

I concurred.

"Very good taste."

I concurred again, whereupon Mr. Cyril Langley delivered the most accurate one-sentence appraisal of T. S. E. that I ever expect to hear:

"Nothing . . . ever . . . quite . . . in excess."

As a tailor, he was perhaps thinking of the Eliotic lapels, a shade wide but not excessively; of the watch chain, a shade massive, but not flamboyantly. I was thinking of effects such as the sudden intrusion of "a patient etherized upon a table" into reveries of evening. Nothing ever quite in excess; yet Eliot's oeuvre, from end to end, does it not career on the brink of excess?

All told, an addition to my education. Once I'd spent an hour with Eliot the role-player, much that I'd found in his poetry was clarified. Even his low-toned last work, the *Four Quartets*, entails an intricate shift from role to role. Suddenly, on the very first page —

My words echo
Thus, in your mind. But to what purpose,
Disturbing the dust on a bowl of rose-leaves,
I do not know . . .[10]

— we catch him in imitation of the ironies of some Harvard lecturer, addressing an apathetic class.

So, those were the modernists I spent time with in Europe. There were other American modernists to be found back in the U.S. Well travelled, they'd elected to base themselves at home. William Carlos Williams, notably: though fluent in French and German, and with a history of time spent abroad both in medical study (he was a doctor) and in cultural tourism, Williams has been typecast as the archetypal American hick, in contrast to the pseudocosmopolitan poet Wallace Stevens, who never in his life left the Western hemisphere.

Williams and Pound had been classmates in Pennsylvania. I visited Williams at his home in Rutherford, New Jersey, not far from the Paterson, NJ, his verse had made famous.

"Is it possible," asked William Carlos Williams, "to

talk with Eliot . . . animal to animal?" What an American question. It's easy to forget that Eliot too was American. In the view of Williams, though, he'd gone over to the enemy, just when an authentic American idiom had a chance of emerging. The American idiom, then, was to be W. C. W.'s sole responsibility, while Eliot enjoyed that maddening dexterity at monopolizing classroom and handbook attention. It's notable that a lecturer, once started on talking about Eliot, does not soon stop, whereas his problems with Williams commence with trying to frame a first sentence.

Williams was born in 1883; when I first visited he was seventy-three and would survive seven more years. The longevity he'd inherited from his mother (who lived to be 102) offset a propensity for strokes that came from his father. So he suffered the strokes, but they didn't kill him. Each one, though, diminished his zones of muscle control, until in his last years the right side of his upper body was paralyzed. When he signed a typescript or a book, very laboriously — always all three names, Wil-liam Car-los Wil-liams — his habit was to grip with his mobile left hand the wrist of his right, which was (somehow) clutching the pen, then to guide the inscription clear across the page.

Very early one morning, as a house-guest on (I think) my last visit to his home, 9 Ridge Road, Rutherford, I was awakened by a loud but insistently irregular "Clack . . . Clack . . . Clack . . ." It was Bill, diligently typing away on the final pages of the poem "Paterson V." He was seated at an early-model IBM Selectric, a retirement gift from the hospital where he'd headed pediatrics for many years. To type each letter — for instance, each of the eight letters in

"Paterson" — his left hand steered his right forefinger over the appropriate key, then let it drop, *Clack*. And the upper-case "P" had to be preceded by a separate manoeuvre towards a "Caps" key, which had next to be turned off. It all took time, much as it had taken Wyndham Lewis time to write all those novels by hand amid total blindness.

Back in about 1948, Williams had written a section for his long poem *Paterson*. Much later, when strokes were having their effect, he installed it as an independent poem in a sequence called *The Desert Music*. There he titled it "The Descent," and we can actually hear its lines descending, stepwise in threes, across a printed page:

> The descent beckons
>   as the ascent beckoned.
>   Memory is a kind
> of accomplishment,
>   a sort of renewal
>   even
> an initiation, since the spaces it opens are new places
>   inhabited by hordes
>   heretofore unrealized. . . .[11]

In Williams's very late work, poem after poem uses the three-step line of "The Descent." There was a good reason for that: by late in life, Williams had difficulty rereading what he had typed. His eyes could easily follow a printed line, but finding where the next line began was a terrible worry. Generally speaking, he could no longer read. (On one of my visits he was preparing to review a reprint of

Chapman's Homer, the book that Keats had memorably looked into. But Williams couldn't "look" into it. I remember his wife, Floss, reading it to him as they sat on a sofa side by side, he leaning towards her low voice, hands clasped between his knees. When had anyone last received Chapman's Homer the way Chapman assumed it would be received: by ear? For in Chapman's time, four centuries ago, it was assumed that verse on a printed page would, as a matter of course, be read aloud.)

Well then, to find the beginning of his typed lines, Williams devised the three-step line. First, he set one left margin and two tab stops and typed his first line at the margin. The next line began one tab stop in. And so on. Williams wrote much verse like that. (Including *Journey to Love*, 1955.) Oddly, no one seems to want to believe that was the reason, though I heard it from Williams himself.

A sequel, finally, to my story of being awakened by the typewriter's slow Clack . . . Clack . . . Clack. That, as it happens, was October 30, 1957, Ezra Pound's seventy-second birthday and the thirty-sixth anniversary to the day of Joyce's finishing *Ulysses*. Bill was seventy-four. And later that momentous morning, say about ten-thirty, I was having coffee downstairs with Floss, when down came Bill bounding, as it were (but it can't have been), two steps at a time, a sheaf of typescript in his left hand. He flung it down in front of me. "There it is! Play with it!" It was "Paterson V," just completed. So I was to be its first reader! (I suggested a few minor cuts, which he made; no, not cuts of his verse, of quoted items merely.)

Williams's writing simply mapped his speech: that was

one insight I gained. It meant that any truly intended utterance will move into poetry. As a doctor, he'd spent hours listening while patients uttered simple words on which their lives, likely, depended. That was unadorned, memorable speech. A Williams poem of 1941 runs, in its entirety,

> Her milk don't seem to . . .
> She's always hungry but . . .
> She seems to gain all right,
> I don't know.[12]

That's surely a verbatim phone call, as is the brief poem that ends, "I don't think it's brea-thin."

⚬

If Bill Williams received you into his domestic bosom, the poet Marianne Moore by contrast, though without Eliot's theatricality, defined a suitable distance. I was never in her famous Brooklyn flat, where visitors were required to take the return subway fare from a bowl of nickels kept just inside the door. (I learned about that from the poet Robert Lowell, who'd been inspired by her example to keep a bowl of coins, for his guests, by the door of his flat in Cambridge, MA: parking meter change. He stopped when he discovered that his bowl, at the end of the month, contained more money than it had thirty days earlier!)

So Marianne Moore defined a suitable distance. Her poems define distance also. Here's something she observed in Brooklyn: a mother bird feeding her young. Listen for the young birds' intermittent "eek":

> Toward the high-keyed intermittent squeak
>   of broken carriage springs, made by
> the three similar meek-
>   coated bird's-eye
> freckled forms she comes, and when
> from the beak
>   of one, the still living
>   beetle has dropped
> out, she picks it up and puts
> it in again.[13]

That is, first of all, a perfectly formal prose sentence.

Also, you need to hear it against the five other stanzas of the poem Moore called "Bird-Witted." Here, for instance, is mating time, when the parent bird sang variations on ute and ote:

>   . . . What delightful note
>   with rapid unexpected flute
> sounds leaping from the throat
>   of the astute
> grown bird, comes back to one from
> the remote
>   unenergetic sun-
>   lit air before
> the brood was here?[14]

There's a final stanza, too, into which a cat intrudes, to gain only frustration. And the whole astonishing achievement (written in 1936) imitates an eleventh-century Provençal poem Ezra Pound had praised four separate times for its skill at matching sound to sense. Miss Moore had been his first reader to respond. That was one of the many reasons I felt I needed to meet her.

In the various environments where I met her, she sat in a chair opposite mine, her hands folded firmly in her lap. She was careful to speak most appreciatively of anything I'd written ("You put that with such finesse!"), but offered nothing about work of her own. And if you'd asked about some local detail you'd have implied a charge of obscurity; so you didn't ask. It was simply up to you to be attentive, to have been attentive, to what was on the page. That was her lesson.

Still, she was always fun to have near. One evening, she turned up at a soirée hosted by a publisher we briefly shared. She was late, because she'd just gotten back to New York from (I think) Bermuda, and ruffled, because in whisking in and out of her flat she'd neglected to bring along money, which had annoyed the taxi driver, whose annoyance in turn annoyed her, because he'd rejected an I.O.U., or a check for any amount, and insisted on immediate cash, which she'd had to borrow from our host. Lord, what an uncivil episode! And how its incivility stood out against her translucent honour! I stooped down to hear about it, amid party din, from under her wide-brimmed hat. (I am six-feet-four, she was tiny and at that time in her seventies.) And it says something about her, that I'm now recalling that encounter as vividly, after several decades, as if it had happened last week.

Then there was the Harvard convention about something or other, at which we were both featured. Robert

Lowell, who knew the Cambridge environment, gathered a few of us for lunch and installed us in his car. Being the only guest of a height comparable to Lowell's, I got the front seat beside him. Back of us, a crowd of four included Marianne Moore, perched upon the bony knees of the poet and critic Allan Tate. That meant that when we'd arrived at the restaurant Marianne was the first to alight, and by the time Lowell had unwound himself from the steering column, she was paying off the parking lot attendant. He: "Marianne, you can't do that!" She: "Oh yes I can."

By the time we were inside, she had located herself at our table in such a way that the waiter would have to pass her to get to Lowell; thus she was able to arrange a separate cheque. You sense a pattern. Yes. (And remember that bowl of subway coins in Brooklyn.) So the next time I was in New York, and she accepted my invitation to lunch, I was prepared to outmanoeuvre her. I ushered her into the booth, then sat beside her; thus I was located between the waiter and Marianne Moore. So it was I who got the cheque, and paid it. That night I was congratulating myself when, just before bed, I discovered that a generous banknote had at some point been slipped into my pocket.

Moral: You cannot hope to win them all.

⁓

Such was the variety — the variousness — of some of the people from whom a literary heritage had come. Apart from Eliot, whose constant concern was that you not find out who he was, they were wonderfully open. (For that, I assign credit to the Pound connection; everyone I saw on that trip had this in common: they greatly respected Ezra Pound.) They are all models to me, as their work should be to all of us. And Elsewhere, though elsewhere, can be gathered in.

We've been discussing writers themselves. Next, we'll discuss how the work of writers, even ancient work, can be gathered in.

IV

THE QUEST FOR
THE PAST

THE AMERICAN POET EZRA Pound, when he was sixty, remembered his Great Aunt Frank taking him to Europe when he was twelve; that would have been in 1898. He wrote poetry about it:

> Cologne Cathedral
> the Torwaldsen lion and Paolo Uccello
> and thence to Al Hambra, the lion court ed el
> mirador de la reina Lindaraja
> orient reaching to Tangier, the cliffs the villa of
> Perdicaris Rais Uli, periplum[1]

In six lines of lean, sparse shorthand, he mapped and preserved their route. We sift through them as we'd search clues for a treasure hunt. Cologne and the great cathedral, the glory of German Gothic; the Torwaldsen lion is a statue in Lucerne, Switzerland, next to the lake; then it was off to Florence, where our clue is Paolo Uccello, his stylized force so unforgettable as to set him apart from all other Florentine painters. Two more names point us to Granada, Spain; and they finally crossed the sea southward to Tangier, the seaport in Morocco.

So Aunt Frank's journey with her nephew was following a then 200-year-old British tradition: that of the Grand Tour, wherein prosperous Britons had "toured the continent." By Aunt Frank's time, prosperous Americans had been at it for about fifty years. Aunt Frank took young Ezra eastward into mid-Europe (Cologne), then southward to Spain, then all the way across the middle sea to North Africa. France, Switzerland, Italy: that had been the traditional Grand Tour itinerary. But now behold, Granada, then Morocco — and with a twelve-year-old for company! These Americans are branching out.

As for the word "periplum" with which the excerpt ends, it's Pound's shorthand for a tour which takes you round and then back. And such a tour is by definition profitable, if not in coins then in knowledge.

Knowledge? Well, listen to a pair of lines from a poem that caught my imagination in high school, the "Ulysses" Alfred Tennyson wrote in 1833:

> To follow knowledge like a sinking star,
> Beyond the utmost bound of human thought.[2]

No, says Tennyson, it does not suffice to stay home.

Humans yearn for knowledge and know it must be sought elsewhere. Tennyson, by the way, was himself following the brilliant example of Dante. In the *Divine Comedy*, written centuries before Tennyson's poem, Dante had the mythical hero Ulysses sailing after knowledge — but more on that later.

Knowledge is of several kinds. When my Siamese cat Francis was twelve weeks old, he saw a tree for the very first time in his life. He promptly scampered over to it and climbed up several feet. That meant (1) recognizing what he saw as something for a cat to climb, and (2) knowing the rather intricate sequence of extending and retracting claws, to get a grip and let go. It's not something he'd ever been taught, even by example. It's innate, inborn knowledge, a spectacular endowment of cats and dogs and horses. Humans have vast innate abilities, mostly abilities to learn: notably, to learn to walk, talk, to learn languages. The innate knowledge of cats is highly specific. And highly mysterious. How on earth did Francis recognize that tree as something to call forth his climbing knowledge?

Then there's the unforeseeable knowledge we gain from journeys, the kind Tennyson had in mind for the Ulysses of his poem to sail after; and that shades into the knowledge we may earn while onlookers imagine we're wasting our time. When Edison was developing his lightbulb, he spent weeks trying out materials for the filament; the first one had been a piece of carbonized thread, which crumbled rather quickly. Someone offered sympathy for the time he was losing. "Not at all," Edison replied, "I now know three hundred things that won't work." A later American inventor, Buckminster Fuller, put that still more briefly: yes, you can always learn more, "but you can't learn less."

Or we can learn by watching transpositions: in 1957 the great *Bugs Bunny* animator, Chuck Jones, issued "What's Opera, Doc?" in which, he likes to claim, we'll find Wagner's twelve-hour, four-opera Ring cycle compressed into six minutes. The film's music was performed by the Burbank Symphony, which was under instructions to avoid any orchestral clowning. And in 1989, at Northwestern University, a professor of music history informed a survey class of music seniors that this week's subject would be the Ring cycle. All forty students promptly burst into a massive rendition of "Kill the wabbit!" They surely weren't mocking Wagner, nor was Bugs Bunny. High and low culture aren't in opposition; the more you know of either, the more you enjoy the other.

So, in Ezra Pound's presentation, he and Aunt Frank, by travelling, had been learning; to what effect, he'd still be meditating nearly five decades later.

And behind their movements we may discern a German publisher named Karl Baedeker, whose red-bound guidebooks to major European cities sought to eliminate the need for guided tours. As the Baedeker books were continually revised, they came to underwrite lists of places one "did," with the tour guide's monologue rising like steam from the page. Always, by convention, the phantom guide addressed a group. You stood where the text told you to, then read "On our left, we see . . ."

By the 1920s, the great Irish novelist James Joyce, commencing his last book, could feel confident that a mere first-person plural pronoun on his printed page would summon the voice of the tour guide. On the very first page of *Finnegans Wake*, sure enough, the eastward run of the river "brings us back . . . to Howth Castle and environs." The "us" says "tour guide," as it will repeatedly throughout the book. We're brought "back" because the first sentence began at the bottom of the book's last page, where after eleven words it broke off to resume at the top of page one. As for Howth Castle, it's on the Hill of Howth which overshadows the north of Dublin Bay. Sure enough, fans of Joyce have been going there ever since.

One Western tradition of sacred places commences with the third chapter of Exodus, where God calls to Moses from a burning bush, "Put off thy shoes from off thy feet, for the place whereon thou standest is holy ground" (Exod. 3:5). God was talking about a holiness there and then, a place that was holy while, and because, He was speaking. The place He designated can no longer be found, let alone named as a lure for pilgrims. But on that model, we've since settled for lists of places we ought to visit because they enshrine some notable event: Mount Sinai, Jerusalem, and Bethlehem are obvious instances. That singling-out custom began with places pilgrims to the Holy Land ought to visit; began, moreover, centuries ago when even then it was risky to go there. It ended with Baedeker lists and their derivatives.

Yet such lists are very old. The list of the Seven Wonders of the World, things that simply had to be seen, dates from the second century B.C.: the Pyramids of Egypt; the Hanging Gardens of Babylon; the statue of Zeus at Olympia; the Temple of Artemis at Ephesus; the Mausoleum at Halicarnassus; the Colossus of Rhodes; the Lighthouse of Alexandria. It was drawn up to celebrate the conquests of Alexander the Great. And what now survives from that particular list? A few ruins, plus the Pyramids. And, of course, an arresting idea . . .

The theme we're circling around is the tour guide's simple directive: Go, Be There. For the tour merchant, these aren't Elsewhere Communities, because they're not communities. They are simply items on a costly agenda. So let us head for, say, the Pyramids of Egypt. And now we confront the Pyramids of Egypt. They are huge, and stony, and resolutely pyramidal, and lo, sure enough they confront us, Pyramids three. And that is that, and hereafter we'll be able to say we've Been There, Done Naught.

Yet it's possible to be drawn into a vanished community, such as that of the people who conceived and worked at such things on such a scale. You may reflect, as my father did a century ago in Rome, that the very dust of Rome's streets "once lived, jested and hated, toiled and battled. Some atoms of that soil made Cicero's lips of eloquence and Caesar's brain of power: all shrivelled and withered now into a few handfuls of wind-driven dust."[3] Such reflections draw on knowledge you take with you: as that God in some early sentences of Genesis made Adam from the dust of the ground; that Shakespeare's Hamlet meditates on conquerors who on dying return to dust; or that the orator Cicero stood for eloquence; and Caesar the warrior for such power as a very few words will summarize. The most quoted sentence of Caesar's consists of just three short Latin words: they say that he came, saw, conquered.

———

You can also get drawn into vanished communities by reading books. That brings us to a story about a story — one of the greatest epics of all time — and how it came to be transmitted to us through a sequence of Elsewhere Communities. It starts with a remarkable German named Heinrich Schliemann. Born in 1822, son of a poor pastor, he was caught up as a schoolboy by a story 2,500 years old: the story Homer, first poet of the West, had told in *The Iliad*, his epic poem about the siege of Troy.

Troy was a great trading city which Greek soldiers attempted to capture for ten years. In Homer's time there was an enormous constellation of stories about the siege and much that came before and after it. Helen, the Greek woman whom we still call "Helen of Troy," had been abducted by Paris, son of the Trojan king. She's been called "the face that launched a thousand ships" because armadas sailed from Greece to fetch her back. That story, and the story of the Trojan Horse, and the story of the escape of Aeneas, the Trojan who sailed westward and founded Rome — all those stories and many more were circulated in Greece in Homer's time. And they are still active in our language today.

Think of the Trojan Horse. It's really the story of the fall of Troy, which finally occurred after the Greeks pretended they'd completely given up their siege. They seemed to have vanished, but were actually hiding behind a nearby island. All they'd left was a giant wooden horse. The Greeks reckoned (rightly) that the pious Trojans would haul that horse in, past the city walls that ten years of siege had never penetrated. So in went the horse, which was stuffed full of Greek warriors, who were able to burst forth and begin the sack of the city.

Today, the expression "Trojan Horse" denotes a covert strategy, such as sneaking unwanted instructions into someone else's computer. Homer used what he needed, from the matter of Troy, for *The Iliad*, his great epic poem about the clash between two heroes, Greek Achilles and Trojan Hector; likewise for *The Odyssey*.

And such was the ring of reality in Homer's language that Heinrich Schliemann believed from his school days to the end of his life that every word was literally true. His driving ambition was to find the site of Troy and dig the city up. It must all be there, for had not Homer said so? Never mind the academic party line of Schliemann's time, that Homer was a poet of brilliant fiction; that there'd never been a Helen, let alone a Troy.

Some years later, Schliemann was rich. He went to a mound called Hissarlik, near the mouth of the Dardanelles, not far from modern Istanbul, and dug. By 1870 he was uncovering remains of a very old burnt city. Troy! (It wasn't, exactly; on that site cities had been repeatedly destroyed and built over; but yes, Homer's Troy had existed on that very site, though Schliemann had dug down past it in his frenzy.) Details could finally be set straight, and they were.

Meanwhile, the theme was established: Homer had celebrated a place that was real, that you could go to and look at. There's a touching story of Schliemann hanging jewels — purported to have been Helen's — on his wife, Sophie, for a photograph.

So yes, Homer had offered, in some guise, fact. And as the archaeological work went on, what had been but sonorous words were coming to denote objects we could touch and handle. For example, the people we call "Greeks" Homer never called "Greeks." He often called them "Achaeans." And he frequently mentioned that they were "well-greaved." The Greeks, it seemed, were well-greaved but the Trojans weren't. Translators intoned the phrase with no idea of what it meant. But now Schliemann and his successors were finding things for the word to pertain to: shin-guards, moreover Achaean artifacts, but never Trojan ones. Hence those "goodly-greaved Achaeans" designated in classrooms. The Greeks were careful of their shins the way modern cricketers are.

In 1860, the poet and critic Matthew Arnold wrote a series of lectures, "On Translating Homer." Unlucky to be writing two decades before Schliemann, Arnold had declared that Homer's verse was a compendium of moral qualities: Homer's style was rapid, he was plain-spoken, he was plain-thinking, he was noble. That he might also be fact-oriented occurred neither to Arnold nor to any other mid-Victorian. Like the Victorian God, the Victorian Homer might well not even have existed, though it did one good to talk as if he had.

The quasi-Biblical manner appears in perfection in

a translation of *The Odyssey* that appeared in 1879 (after Schliemann, true, but the translators didn't seem to know it):

> . . . unless it so be that my father, the goodly Odysseus,
> out of evil heart wrought harm to the goodly-greaved
> Achaeans,
> in quittance whereof ye now work me harm out of evil
> hearts . . .

So impenetrable was the diction, not to mention the syntax, that a puzzler like "goodly-greaved" would likely slip by unremarked. That was one secret of Victorian translators.

Something else was happening in the post-Schliemann years. Homer, in other centuries, had been above all the poet of *The Iliad*. But for about a decade after 1900, he became, first and foremost, the poet of *The Odyssey*. That was because the homegoing of Odysseus entails adventures and misadventures around much of the Mediterranean world. What should have taken him perhaps a matter of weeks occupied fully ten years amid endless detours and delays. And just as there'd been a real Troy, so there'd likely been real places for the Sirens, the Cyclops, the Lotus-Eaters, the magician Circe — all of them providing adventures for Odysseus.

It now seemed feasible to locate these places. For if Homer — traditionally blind — had not explored the Mediterranean on his own, he must have depended on accounts by voyagers who had: Phoenician traders, for instance. In 1903, a French scholar named Victor Berard published a book about the Phoenicians and *The Odyssey*:

a meticulous canvassing of detail. It found its way into the hands of James Joyce, whose huge 1922 novel, *Ulysses*, reflects the Homer of the post-Schliemann years. It's an odyssey within the city of Dublin, occupying not years but a single day. And it's full of implicit dialogue with archaeologists to come, in perhaps 2,000 years.

Much of what you can excavate from an archaeological site consists of the trash its inhabitants once discarded — the broken dishes, the kitchen debris. And thanks to Homeric texts, we can now supply names for the objects so excavated. Likewise, archaeologists of A.D. 4000, tunnelling through the remains of Dublin, may find what's left of a kitchen at what was once Number 7 Eccles Street. And in that kitchen, a china cup with a little shelf across half the width of its mouth. And "Eureka!" an analyst on the team may cry, reflecting (1) that a recorded one-time frequenter of that kitchen, named Leopold Bloom, sported a moustache, and (2) that it may have been the purpose of that little shelf to keep the ends of his moustache out of his tea. And the immortal text, James Joyce's *Ulysses*, contains, does it not, in connection with that very kitchen, the phrase "moustache cup"? True, it's hardly the most spectacular relic of early twentieth-century Dublin, but at least one for which we now have a name and a purpose supplied.

Joyce is scrupulously naming real objects, just as Homer did. He's also well aware that Homer's objects were actually found, in the age of Schliemann, by diggers who learned from Homer what those objects were called. And we can see how Joyce is playing a game with future archaeologists of Dublin when that city in turn gets dug up in a couple of millennia (*Ulysses* surviving, of course, the way Homer's epics have). With all that in mind, we can derive great amusement from the lists towards the end of *Ulysses*, lists of the contents of drawers and cupboards (a birth certificate, a bank passport, a pair of convex horn-rimmed spectacles . . .). Those strings of names are obviously meant for the convenience of those coming archaeologists. *Ulysses* is a book you frequent the way you'd frequent a community.

In short, the Homer behind James Joyce's *Ulysses* — which I think is the most influential book in English since *Paradise Lost* — is the Homer after Schliemann: a Homer with an accurate and tireless eye for exact, material detail.

Besides Schliemann's, there are other stories about how Homer has come down to us, in one form or another. For instance, there's the story that starts with the poet Dante, in Italy in the fourteenth century. We rightly think of Homer as the beginning of European literature; yet for many centuries Homer went unread in Western Europe, simply because almost no one was left there who could read Greek. Latin was Western Europe's universal language, and it was a language into which Homer had not been translated.

Dante knew of Homer, by reputation. He also knew a story about a hero named Ulysses, which is a Latinized version of Odysseus, the hero of Homer's *Odyssey*. And in his *Inferno*, Dante tells us how he met Ulysses, who describes how he himself had died. He'd finally gotten home from Troy, but then he'd grown restless; for nothing, Ulysses says,

Could conquer the inward hunger that I had
To master earth's experience, and to attain
Knowledge of man's mind: both the good and the bad.[4]

Ulysses as a man with a lust for knowledge: that seemed appropriate in Italy's High Middle Ages; never mind that the Odysseus of Homer had simply wanted to get home and stay there. (Dante's, by the way, is also the Ulysses we were talking about earlier, the one Tennyson contrived five centuries later.)

And that's not the end of the story. Dante also took up one of Homer's major themes, without, it seems, knowing it came from Homer himself. That is the Journey to the Land of the Dead. In his *Divine Comedy*, Dante divided the realm of the dead into three parts: Hell (the Inferno), Purgatory, and Paradise. He was certainly aware that he was Christianizing an idea he'd found in the sixth book of the *Aeneid*, the great epic poem by Vergil, who wrote in Latin a thousand years before Dante wrote in Italian. In his book, Vergil takes his hero Aeneas down among the shades with three famous words about how easy it is to get there — "Facilis descensus Averno." It is, after all, something everyone born on this earth will accomplish. To return, though, that is the trick: Hic labor, hic opus est. Well, Aeneas had famously managed the return, and Dante will now have us know that he did too. Which seemed a neat pairing. Dante even takes Vergil as his guide.

But what Dante got from Vergil, Vergil of course had gotten from Homer, whose *Iliad* and *Odyssey* Vergil knew well. In his day, educated Romans read Greek. Latin was the vulgar tongue. And so, Dante seems not to have known that Homer described a journey to the Land of the Dead before him. It's in the eleventh book of *The Odyssey* where Homer takes his hero, Odysseus, to the shades to consult the ghost of Tiresias, the greatest prophet of the Homeric world. Odysseus gets the advice he went after, returns to the land of the living, and resumes his voyage.

Dante died in 1321; 217 years later, there was at last a Latin version of Homer. How delighted Dante would have been to read the actual *Odyssey* for himself, to find the roots of his own Ulysses, his own Journey to the Underworld! On the shoulders of giants, indeed.

By the early sixteenth century, printed books were ubiquitous, and you could get a Greek *Odyssey* that would slip into your pocket. Travel in his coach offered plenty of time for a well-off and educated man to study it; but lacking Greek dictionaries — and there were none — he'd need help with the words. In 1538 help was provided, by someone who signed himself Andreas Divus Justinopolitanus. His helper would also slip into a pocket. It was simply a page-for-page, line-for-line translation into Latin, the tongue in which all the literate were fluent. Stuck by the third word, seventh line, page 148? Just turn to the corresponding word in Divus!

And late in the first decade of the twentieth century, the American poet Ezra Pound, himself a frequenter of Elsewhere Communities, was ambling down a Paris quai where he chanced upon a copy of Divus. Pound had never

before read Homer in Latin. The experience led him to make
connections that would profoundly affect his own writing.

Book Eleven, he thought, the story of Odysseus visiting
the Land of the Dead, was probably the oldest material in
The Odyssey — hence the beginning of known Greek literature. And in the Latin translation by Divus he saw
something equally momentous: an event that had helped
launch the Renaissance, that prodigious rebirth of classic
art, literature, and learning. Pound set out to pass on the
Homeric tradition he'd received from so many sources.

He took an Anglo-Saxon poem, "The Seafarer," one of
the earliest poems written in England. It's the story of a sea
voyage. It can also be read as an allegory of Man the
Pilgrim, exiled from Paradise, a wanderer on Earth. Pound
used it to launch his own magnum opus, *The Cantos*. There
he blended four sources, superimposing four beginnings:
of Greek literature, of poetry written in England, of the
Renaissance, and of his own work.

> And then went down to the ship,
> Set keel to breakers, forth on the godly sea, and
> We set up mast and sail on that swart ship,
> Bore sheep aboard her, and our bodies also,
> Heavy with weeping, and winds from sternward
> Bore us out onward with bellying canvas,
> Circe's this craft, the trim-coifed goddess.
> Then sat we amidships, wind jamming the tiller,
> Thus with stretched sail, we went over sea till day's end[5]

"And then went down to the ship"?: what's this, a long

book that begins with "And"? No, we don't confront some headstrong modernist mannerism. Pound is reproducing the way Divus opens his version of *The Odyssey* XI with the Latin word "at," which means "and." And Divus is following the Greek word "Autar" — "moreover" — with which Homer begins Book Eleven of his *Odyssey*.

"Thus with stretched sail, we went over sea till day's end." Out, then, over the sea, which for all Greek geographers know, may well be infinite. So it's the same sea Odysseus travelled. And now, we are following instructions from Circe, a slippery goddess indeed. For right at the beginning of *The Cantos*, we're entering the ancient, classical, literary tradition. Circe has told Odysseus that if he really means to get home, he must first visit the Underworld. And if we wish for significant poetry in our own time, we must first visit and absorb that long tradition.

Vergil's Aeneas also had to learn from the dead. Vergil was bringing his hero all the way from Troy to what would be the site of Rome, to perform heroic deeds that would render Rome possible: . . . genus unde Latinum, Albanique patres, atque altae moenia Romae — whence the Latin race, and the Alban fathers, and the high walls of Rome.

And the High Walls of Rome: atque *al*tae *moe*nia Romae; how vividly I remember the classicist Gilbert Norwood, at the University of Toronto, banging the seminar table to bring forth those metrical stresses! So Vergil's pulse could affect an alien nervous system nearly two millennia later.

And so our insatiable hunger for knowledge — what Dante's Ulysses sailed after, what Dante's Aristotle personified — continues to transcend time and space.

"Maestro di color che sanno," Dante called Aristotle: the master of those who know. Time and Space. And now, at the threshold of the twenty-first century, our hunger for knowledge is beginning to transcend even our physical bodies, in still newer ways. We'll be exploring that possibility in our last talk.

V

AND NOW, THE
INVISIBLE TOURIST

THE ELSEWHERE COMMUNITY WE'VE been talking about is not
so much an ideal we can define, as it is a set of instances we
can point to. They are instances of human collaboration,
which can sometimes even be unconscious, or else as simple
and sustaining as the knowledge that we're not alone.

At one extreme, we've seen the young Irish poet Paddy
Kavanagh, walking eighty miles southward from his farm
to visit the elder poet George William Russell, who went
by the name of AE. But AE sent Paddy back home with
sixty-odd pounds of books. And the Elsewhere Community
in which Paddy was soon immersed consisted of his memories of AE's generous hospitality and also much that was
in those books. Later, a transformed Kavanagh would
become an Elsewhere Community for a younger generation of poets in whom he'd breed the hope that though

they, too, were provincials, they might have something to write about.

At another extreme, we've seen the poet Ezra Pound collaborating with the poet T. S. Eliot on the revision of Eliot's seminal twentieth-century poem, *The Waste Land*. Ezra Pound marked passages for deletion, from whole typed pages down to single lines. He noted that the rhythm of this or that sequence was monotonously "tum-tum," which spurred Eliot to great prodigies of revision. Pound also rejected the anxious Eliot's feeling that the whole thing needed a prelude. And finally, he accepted Eliot's dedication: to Ezra Pound, "il miglior fabbro" — a phrase Dante had used in the *Divine Comedy*, meaning "the better craftsman." Pound and Eliot: that was an interaction of poets different but equal. Both, in fact, American, but very different in background and temperament. Each of them offered an Elsewhereness for the other.

When he was very young, Pound vowed that by age thirty he'd know more about the writing of poetry than anyone else living. What he probably didn't foresee was a dual vocation, Poet and Mentor; Elsewhere Communities lend themselves to mentoring. In about 1912, Pound came into a modest sum of money. He promptly bought two pieces of sculpture from an artist he admired, and also his first typewriter. For the rest of his life, he'd spend hours of many days typing: sometimes up to thirty copies of the same letter, in, say, six batches of five, using carbon paper. The copies were meant for a shifting inventory of people he was mentoring. Pound could certainly have used what technology had not yet supplied: the photocopy machine.

Put to such continuous use, a typewriter would normally last Pound about three years.

For years then, Ezra Pound mentored people who lived Elsewhere. But not all of us are fortunate enough to correspond with our mentors. Let alone meet them. My father, for instance, never met his. They were dead. But he was able to visit the place they had lived.

In 1898, when my father went abroad — as was expected of all good high school teachers — he was, in effect, re-enacting that long-standing tradition and invention: the Grand Tour to the continent. Specifically to Rome. And while in Rome, he passionately reflected that the dust on the streets might still contain atoms that once made Cicero's "lips of eloquence," or Caesar's "brain of power." Afterwards, my father conveyed that passion to generations of students. Unfortunately, the costs of travel being what they were, he never returned to Europe.

To generalize: the life of the mind, and the fulfilment of the person, these are the rewards of participating in a community. And because we learn most from people who've experienced things we haven't, the most fulfilling communities have lain elsewhere. Not that it's always necessary to pack one's bags. The poet John Milton celebrated "the precious life-blood of a master spirit, embalmed and treasured up on purpose to a life beyond life."[1] He was talking about "a good book." And the poet Keats spoke of having "much travell'd in the realms of gold."[2] He was referring to the world of books. Yes, the book and its reader do share a community, with this restriction: if the reader talks to the author, the author cannot respond. Full two-way interaction — person-to-person/in-person — is something tourism makes possible.

But here we are, and it's 1997; and lo, near the very turn of the millennium, we're hearing that tourism may grow obsolete. And what could oust it? Well, there's talk of an electronic Elsewhere Community: universal — planet-wide - - communication, no less. All knowledge everywhere instantly accessible, all expertise at everybody's service. I speak, of course, of a phenomenon known as the Internet. Why drag yourself through costly and tiresome journeys, now that you can enjoy their benefits when you choose, viewing your console from a comfortable chair in your very own home, and tapping your keyboard after due reflection?

The Internet is the fastest growing technology in history, but it's not universally available yet. And I think it's worth emphasizing just how vague the numbers are. "Planet-wide communication" means, in practice, that Internet connections are restricted to that subset of the planetary population with both access to affordable computers and interest in using them. Moreover, the Internet situates us in a world where many addresses can lead back to a single person, whom a compiler of numbers could easily mistake for six or seven different people. Then there's a frequent multiplicity of machines per person; I myself currently use three, each of which has Internet access, though I'm not on the Internet via more than one machine at a time. And I'm also reachable via my employer, a large university. An incautious survey that equated an address-count or a machine-count with a head-count could easily multiply my presence by four. Many surveys err in that way.

Still, a pretty reliable estimate places the count of Internet users worldwide at perhaps sixty million, maybe half of them in the U.S., the rest mainly in other Western countries. Placing that against a planetary population of some six billion souls, we gather that maybe one human in a thousand has Internet experience. The proportion could double or triple or quadruple without amounting to a global takeover.

And by the way, just as the Internet — an "electronic" Elsewhere Community — has its limitations at present (you need time, money, and interest), so the Grand Tour back in the eighteenth century had its limitations as well. The Grand Tour was a way of getting from, say, England to an actual Elsewhere Community, probably in Rome. And you needed interest, yes, but also time (months or years), and money (lots of money). And you still had problems the Internet doesn't present. When the British writer Horace Walpole crossed the Alps en route to Rome in about 1740, he took with him his King Charles Spaniel, named Tory. He incautiously let Tory out of the carriage to relieve himself, whereupon Tory was eaten by a wolf. No, there seems to be no Internet equivalent. Unless of course, you count computer viruses.

So, the Net is far from netting the globe. That's not to discount its importance. For one thing, it's very active as a reference library as well as a space where persons interact. That was once an explicit distinction. You walked into the library, and asked a question of the person behind the desk. An answer directed you to where the relevant books were. You took volumes down, flipped their pages; should the search dead-end you'd return to the reference desk. But eventually you closed in on your quarry. Then you made a few notes and walked out.

But today, in Chaucer's resonant word, "Namoor!" The desk is now in your home or office, not the library. And you can't actually see the librarians, though they do exist. They call themselves "web-masters." They work away — all over the world — sorting through all the data that eventually ends up on the Internet. They organize it and "post" it. And as for books, there are millions available on the Internet, but it's fair to say that books in themselves are largely overshadowed, even outweighed, by information. Data. In the form of "databases." Last summer a compendium of nine million references and abstracts from 4,000 medical journals became available free to Internet users. Soon the Medline website was receiving one million visits a day. "Americans," one commentator remarked, "are consuming medical information as if it were candy."[3]

To back off a little: the Internet is a huge Elsewhere Community, though perhaps uniquely vulnerable to all manner of abuse. It has other unique features. A few weeks ago, a chance opening of a magazine presented me with a photograph of a man I've regarded for six years or so as a friend. We've exchanged hundreds of Internet messages, and twice he's parcel-posted me videotapes he thought I ought to see. Those tapes fed my work on a book, which I dedicated to him. And never, till seeing that photo, have I had an idea of what he looked like. (An engaging smile, on a face much younger than I'd expected.) I still don't know how his voice sounds. Moreover, the department of the

Internet where he and I correspond, called BIX, for the Byte Information Exchange (founded some years ago by *BYTE* magazine), affords me contact with other friends as well. I've only met three of them in person. One of them is a physician, who periodically e-mails me advice on what sort of specialist I should seek out. His own practice is based more than a thousand miles from where I live.

This is not the way we normally meet people. In a non-electronic world, speech comes after sight, and written words after words heard, which in turn come after rituals of introduction — "Jim, I'd like you to meet my friend Don" — that lack any Net equivalent. On the Net, one of two parties takes the initiative, prompted by some sign of common interest. Yes, tales abound of role-playing; of ostensibly lissome young women who are really middle-aged men. But that's not what I'm talking about; I'm talking about sincere communication that — at least for now — depends neither on sight nor sound. It's an entirely new order of human experience.

What about letters? Ah, but letters you send through the mail usually follow the traditional rituals of acquaintance-ship: you meet in person; you maintain the friendship by mail. Moreover, postal mail takes time — at least overnight — whereas a Net to-and-fro can involve a dozen messages or so in a quarter of an hour. And that's a major difference. Communicating as quickly as the Net permits resembles the give-and-take of conversation, something no post office ever pretended to offer. When we talk, what you say is partly shaped by the knowledge that what I just said still hovers in my mind; as also, more remotely, my mind holds echoes of whatever it was I said. But a letter: that refers to a document I'm looking at as I write it, back beyond which, well, we're talking of filing systems, maybe even secretaries. So the Net is informal in a fundamental way that not even a "Dear Jim" letter can aspire to.

And so we find the internationally syndicated columnist Judith Martin, otherwise known as "Miss Manners," approving what is becoming a Net convention: first-name greetings, first-name signatures. She's right that they help remedy the electronic remoteness. She also offers the arresting observation that young techies on the Net "know more about etiquette than their parents' generation." ("Oh, not more than Miss Manners, of course," she hastens to add. "They're only human ")[4] Her point is, in forming new types of communities, they've grown aware of etiquette "as an essential factor in community life." How not to be a bore? When should a duo free up other people's time by shifting its conversation to a private space? Where is the line between joking and vulgarity? Between friendliness and prying? In a sidebar, Miss Manners also quotes the *Wall Street Journal*, to the effect that, as the Internet expands, some pioneers are abandoning it out of weariness with growing incivility. Alas, "the bigger the network community gets, the more it behaves like society as a whole."[5] The whole subject has a name. It's "netiquette."

Still, it's extremely hard to make generalizations about the Internet, let alone predictions. And because it's all so new, people of my generation tend to think we won't be around to see what it's really all about. We're also encouraged to think of the Net as a young folks' medium. In the

Acknowledgements to her recent book on cyberspace, Janet Murray, who has taught at MIT for a quarter-century and founded a Laboratory for Advanced Technology there, is thanking her teenaged son "who has served as my trusty Internet sleuth, and whose bountiful imagination and keen literary intelligence were my constant companion through all the labyrinthine tangles of this investigation." A lad serving as Mom's torch through the labyrinth: yes, that's a familiar image. Yet the same day I read that, I lighted on a nationwide survey concerning older adults and computers. Computer ownership among college graduates aged seventy-five and older? Fifty-three percent! Now that is startling. Eighty-four percent of those engage in writing, word processing, and e-mail; fifty-four percent in managing finances; thirty-four percent in graphics and desktop publishing; and, oh yes, sixty percent in games.

"The mature market, with more disposable income and spare time than other age groups, also spends the most time on home computers: 12 hours a week." Here's a retired English professor in Georgia whose son went out and bought the computer, "But I found the Pathfinder address before he did." She now uses it for everything you can think of. "She e-mails her son and daughter-in-law in North Carolina daily, faxes items to her church committees, helps her husband produce financial statements for his civic clubs, visits health and travel sites on the World Wide Web, keeps tabs on Oprah Winfrey's book club, and writes large-print, bold-type letters to her mother. 'My mother is ninety-two and she has remarked that she doesn't know what kind of big typewriter I've got now, but she certainly does like it.'"[6]

Another Georgian, age eighty-two, marvels at the Internet's limitless variety: "Trouble is, I'm hopping around from one thing to another like a bumblebee buzzing from flower to flower. I don't know when to stop."[7]

And a sixty-eight-year-old from North Carolina "Maintains his own home page as well as the Web site for his Masonic lodge, sends e-mail, buys books from a Seattle store, plays duplicate bridge with partners in Japan, participates in beta testing for software developers, and dispatches letters to the editor of his newspaper."[8]

Contrary to popular belief, cyberspace is filled with senior citizens. The Internet is not solely a young person's medium. And what's more, it's the "virtualness" of the medium that opens up the Net to everybody: there are no physical limitations. This is spectacular if you think of the Internet in light of, say, other kinds of journeys humans have taken in the past: physical journeys, like the Grand Tour to the continent. Those who went on that journey to Elsewhere were visibly mostly young. They were also visibly rich; and visibly mostly male. Today, the Internet has changed the rules of the game. At least for virtual travel. Democratized it, as it were.

There is another aspect of the Internet we haven't touched on yet: the way the Internet changes our relationship to mentor figures in our lives. To get at this idea, I'd like to talk a bit about R. Buckminster Fuller. He was a dominant figure of the early twentieth century, though the century was slow to realize that.

Born in 1895, Buckminster Fuller was conscious all his long life of being the grand-nephew of Margaret Fuller, the wise lady respected by Ralph Waldo Emerson, America's foremost nineteenth-century sage. Bucky (as he was known) had inherited her desk, and at moments of crisis he'd repair to it and sit there, pressing his fingers to his brow.

Bucky Fuller is remembered for the geodesic domes he invented. Molecular science has also recently immortalized his name with the "buckminsterfullerene": that's an assemblage of geodesic-shaped molecules Bucky had foreseen. They were not fully realized in his lifetime. But perhaps he was best known for his platform performances from, say, 1940 until his death in 1983. Those were the years — a generation ago — when Bucky was in full visibility. He zoomed around the globe in person, bearing his news to audiences in town after town after town. He wore three watches, to tell him (1) the time back home, (2) the time where he was now, and (3) the time at his next stop. In his seventies, he switched from buying cars to renting them, having discerned a too-often repeated pattern of a car forgotten at the previous airport. Wherever he touched down he gathered in crowds, sometimes so large that the overflow had his discourse piped to satellite auditoriums. And the discourse might go on for up to four or five mesmerizing hours.

There was no substitute for Bucky Fuller's actual presence. Much depended on gesture. "Why," my little daughter once asked him, "is the fire hot?" They were sitting in front of a fireplace, crackling logs, leaping flames. Taking her onto his lap, Bucky bade her remember a tree, and as he did so, he impersonated a tree — I almost said, turned into a tree — his outstretched arms and fingers gathering, gathering. This tree, he said, spent its life gathering in the sunlight. Then, cut down, it was sawed into logs. "What you see," he concluded, indicating the fireplace, "is the sunlight, unwinding from the log." As it was. And little Lisa understood perfectly.

On the Internet, that exposition would lose much, notably, a tender moment in front of the fire and the physical presence of what was being explained. Still, the Net offers something one-on-one presence does not: access to any mentor who has a computer, anywhere in the world. Media always offers gains, though offset by losses.

It's useful, I think, to sort certain benefits of technology under two headings: "Going" versus "Just Looking." "Going" took people somewhere: Paddy Kavanagh on foot to Dublin, my father by steamship and train to Rome. The history of "Going" reaches far back, to the first stirring of people from their home communities: to hunt, to gather, to meet other people, see other places. "Just Looking" is what a different technology enables: the TV, for instance, the computer screen. Those show you a lot, granted, but it comes to you with a hidden cost, since your contact with what you are shown is sharply limited.

The telephone and the radio offer a more intimate experience than does the TV; that's because so much of human identity resides in the voice. The most creative way to look is to listen. Charles Dickens, in the nineteenth century, wrote his novels on the assumption that the pages would be read aloud within a family. He himself drew crowds to his own public readings of his most intense passages. It's said that when he'd finished reading the famously pathetic death scene of Little Nell (the heroine of *The Old Curiosity Shop*) there wasn't a dry eye left in the house. But reading aloud is little practised now, except for that relatively new phenomenon, the audiobook, which is useful for people who are blind. They're also marketed so you can absorb some reading while you drive your car.

To stress the advantages of listening is in no way to dismiss what the Internet's screen can bring. I once needed a source for a mathematical topic. I had no idea where to look it up, or how. So I put a query on BIX. Within three hours, someone in India came through with the answer: the journal I needed had been published, decades ago, in Sweden. Bingo!

I should also mention that computers are now equipped with sound and pictures. You can hear radio programs on the Internet. And you can see pictures: graphics, photographs, videos, the news — anything you can put on television, you can put onto the Internet. To say nothing of things you can't put on television! You can even "C-U-C-ME": talk to someone in real time and see them in real time, over the Internet. A telephone with pictures. Live conferencing. My own computer is not equipped with any of this — Lord knows where it will lead us.

Meanwhile, there's always a pessimistic slant. An Atlanta columnist guesses that the Net "will follow the same scenario as commercial radio and television." That means, logons you now pay for "will be subsidized by folks who are eager for you to tune in." And sadly, "when popular tastes set the standards, you can expect to see the Cyber equivalents of the mindlessness of commercial radio and television."[9] "Folks who are eager for you to tune in" are, alas, folks ready and willing to sell you something. In short, the whole point of the Net is changing. It started as a decentralized technology: we all had a piece of it — or thought we did. But now, a lot of people are eager to stake out and claim big chunks of it for themselves. For the time being, the question remains: from whom would they buy it? For no one owns the Internet yet. No, not even Bill Gates.

In a recent *Times Literary Supplement*, Alberto Manguel, the author of a fascinating book published in 1996 called *A History of Reading*, offered a comparison between his own experience of reading today and that of St. Augustine in the fourth century A.D. Let me quote several sentences:

> For Augustine, the words on the page — not the perishable scroll or the replaceable codex that held them — had physical solidity, a burning, visible presence. For me, the solidity is in the expensive edifice of the computer, not in the fleeting words. . . . This accounts for the difference in the vocabulary used by Augustine and by myself to describe the act of reading. Augustine spoke of "devouring" or "savouring" a text — a gastronomical image derived from a passage in Ezekiel. I instead speak of "surfing" the web, of "scanning" a text. For Augustine,

the text has a material quality that requires ingestion.
For the computer reader, the text exists only as a surface
which is "skimmed," as he rides the waves of information from one cyber-area to another.[10]

The passage in Ezekiel about "devouring" and "savour-
ing" a text is from Ezekiel 3:3, where a voice from heaven
instructs the prophet to absorb a scroll:

> Son of man, cause thy belly to eat, and fill thy bowels
> with this roll that I give thee. Then did I eat it; and it
> was in my mouth as honey for sweetness.

He's next sent out to admonish the House of Israel. That's
the sort of thing that was meant when the Jews were called
"the People of the Book." The idea is continued in the 1548
injunction of the English Book of Common Prayer, that all
should "read, mark, and inwardly digest." But try to designate "People of the Web" and the metaphor evaporates.
We don't speak of "digesting" scraps of electronic mail. It's
skimmed, deleted, filed (even perhaps saved).

And yet, the need for Elsewhere Communities still
abides. It's been present ever since humans began to move
a little distance from the field near which they were born.
Once, Europe's population was mostly peasantry. (The
Oxford English Dictionary identifies a "peasant" by his
adherence to his plot of land.) But by the Renaissance some
people were in motion. And by the eighteenth century,
as we saw earlier, many more were heading Elsewhere,
along routes defined by facilities for moving travellers in

numbers. And so, we looked at the ways people crossed the Alps: history having defined Italy, specifically Rome, as the mecca of northern Europeans — the English, the French, the Germans. But finally, there arrived the historic moment, unforgettably defined by the poet William Wordsworth, when the sheer experience of crossing the Alps came to transcend Rome or whatever else lay south of them. Listen again to Wordsworth, overwhelmed by wonders he never dreamed of:

> . . . The immeasurable height
> Of woods decaying, never to be decayed,
> The stationary blasts of waterfalls, . . .
> The torrents shooting from the clear blue sky,
> Black drizzling clouds that spake by the way-side . . .
> Tumult and peace, the darkness and the light —
> Were all like workings of one mind, the features
> Of the same face, blossoms upon one tree;
> Characters of the great Apocalypse,
> The types and symbols of Eternity,
> Of first, and last, and midst, and without end.[11]

And so, the traveller became his own community, seeking wonders in nature that could be experienced alone: experienced internally through the inward eye of solitude. Nearly a century of Romantic individualism was introduced.

When William Wordsworth returned to northwestern England, he wrote poem after poem about fascinating but solitary encounters with nature: as with a field of daffodils ("I gaz'd and gaz'd"[12]) the memory of which returned to comfort him in his times of vacancy. And yet, only this past summer, in its weekly competition to identify authors, the *Times Literary Supplement* offered the following quotation. And guess who wrote it?

> We are pleased with what we have seen in our travels. We intend to import into England a new invention for washing. Among other advantages which our patent will set forth we shall not fail to insist upon the immense saving which must result from our discovery which will render only one washing bason necessary for the largest family in the kingdom. We dare not trust this communication to a letter, but you shall be a partner.[13]

Give up? The date turns out to be February 27, 1799. The letter is addressed to the poet and critic S. T. Coleridge, and the part just quoted is in the handwriting of William Wordsworth himself! So Coleridge was to be partner to William and Dorothy (William's sister), in a scheme for improving the estate of the Great Unwashed; and that was to be the breathlessly imparted fruit of a European trip.

No more seems to have been heard of the "washing bason" project. It's unnecessary to specify what else we've gained from Wordsworth's travels, verse of the order of

> a sense sublime
> Of something far more deeply interfused,
> Whose dwelling is the light of setting suns,
> And the round ocean and the living air,

And the blue sky, and in the mind of man:
A motion and a spirit, that impels
All thinking things, all objects of all thought,
And rolls through all things. . . .[14]

That was composed on a tour to Wales, by a man who was far from a stay-at-home. And had T. S. Eliot stayed in Cambridge, Massachusetts, we'd not have *The Waste Land*. But for James Joyce's separation from the Dublin of 1904, taking his vivid memories of the city with him to Trieste, Zurich, and to Paris, no *Ulysses*. And if Ezra Pound had settled down in his first teaching job, in Crawfordsville, Indiana, we'd have been unspeakably deprived.

Great writers have always needed an Elsewhere Community. Dante worked not in Florence but in a penal exile that distanced him from Florence. And if for Shakespeare it sufficed simply to move without melodrama from Stratford to London (in his day a major upheaval), well, we're fortunate. Shakespeare heard and saw things that later he would remember and write about in his plays. And what he heard near home and put into words, printers would one day kill for: Shakespeare had collected pebbles and showed us they were diamonds.

A few years ago, a friend of mine was visiting England. In Stratford, he saw a farmer gently blowing off the top of a dandelion that had gone to seed. "We call these golden lads chimney-sweepers when they come to dust," the farmer told my friend. (Think of the sweeper's brush the grey dandelion resembles; or the dust that drifts away when it is blown.) And in *Cymbeline*, a play Shakespeare wrote in about 1611, we read solemn words about Death the Leveller:

Golden lads and girls all must,
As chimney sweepers, come to dust.[15]

One need not think of a dandelion to be moved by those dozen words, as London audiences were moved some four hundred years ago; as we are still moved today. The American poet Robert Frost used to compare the effect of poetry to the effect of talk we hear from the next room, situating such words as we can recognize amid patterns of pace and pitch and emphasis. Yes, language came over like that; "golden" will fit "lads and girls" without the aid of a flower.

And as the local leaves its marks on the universal, the reverse can also happen. Much effort has gone into reconstructing the psychic biography of Shakespeare from his Sonnets; but Ezra Pound once remarked to me that the Shakespeare of the Sonnets may well have been "a public letter-writer": that's writing poetry-to-order — a trade. Pound told me this during the time he was imprisoned in a mental hospital in Washington D.C. "Sometimes," he added, "the guards come to me, for a piece of verse to give their sweethearts." "And do you write it?" I asked. "Oh, yes." In Hampstead, London, England, 1956, I saw a tree that had been carefully labelled, "This tree replaces the tree under which Keats wrote 'Ode to a Nightingale.'" It's doubtful a Washington madhouse will ever be similarly designated.

Still, people, feeling they're Elsewhere, will feel they

should reach out. Most North American cities, including Peterborough, the Canadian city where I grew up, have a Euclid Avenue, so named by the surveyors who laid them out and were careful to leave behind the name of the master of geometry who is the patron saint of surveyors. And across the top of New York state, how did all those classical city-names come about? Troy, Ilion, Ithaca . . . And for that matter, I live in Athens, Georgia, a pleasant city not far from Sparta, Georgia.

Statistics just a few decades ago were confirming that a man was most likely to marry the girl next door. That grows rarer today, so much do North Americans shift ground. (A Canadian, I've been happy for over thirty years with a wife from Maryland whom I met in Virginia, and today we live in Georgia.) Travel has grown far simpler, far cheaper, and we all sense many ways to fulfil the need for an Elsewhere. It's pointless to complain of rootlessness, restlessness. We enter not merely the much-heralded cyberspace, but also a physical future, potentially welcome for all of us.

This Elsewhere combines both virtual and actual presences: all the sorts of things that have populated these talks. They include physical journeys to an Elsewhere in which, like Grand Tour denizens flocking to Rome, we can imaginatively join communities of the past, and notably a past in which we can say our present culture has its roots. And they include great thinkers and artists of our own time, who irresistibly draw us into their communities, which illuminate our own communities. None of us can ever know when we ourselves may be fulfilling, in our normal lives, the role of Elsewhere for some visitor we may chance to meet.

In the communities we've been exploring, there is no distinction between high and low culture. There's no high culture because there's no other culture that needs to be set aside as low.

And so James Joyce in *Ulysses* takes his Leopold Bloom past a shop window — Brown Thomas, on Grafton Street, Dublin — that contains a display of ladies' underthings. A sudden erotic onrush ensues, conveyed by two sentences Joyce spent a day's work on:

> Perfume of embraces all him assailed. With hungered flesh obscurely, he mutely craved to adore.[16]

A day's work on two sentences? "Yes," Joyce responded, "I had the words. What I was working at was the order of the fifteen words in the sentences. There is an order in every way exact. I think I have found it."[17]

And with Joyce counting words, compare the story of the great *Bugs Bunny* animator, Chuck Jones, sending the Coyote repeatedly over the cliff as yet one more scheme for trapping the Roadrunner goes awry. Before he hits the bottom, Jones determined, eighteen frames should elapse. More or fewer would be less effective, and Jones claimed that an error of two frames more or less was quite detectable. We're talking about a margin for error of a twelfth of a second. Word-count, frame-count, that is a mode of consciousness peculiar to our century.

It's a consciousness governed by a passion. Yes, passion.

And passion is the note to end on. It's our passions we are remembered by. Joyce's passion for exactness has kept *Ulysses* readable for three quarters of a century now. And thanks to Jones's analogous passion, six-minute cartoons he and his crew made in the 1930s and '40s continue to fascinate us in the 1990s.

Yes, "What thou lovest well remains," wrote Ezra Pound:

What thou lovest well remains,

       the rest is dross
What thou lov'st well shall not be reft from thee
What thou lov'st well is thy true heritage
Whose world, or mine or theirs

      or is it of none?
First came the seen, then thus the palpable
  Elysium, though it were in the halls of hell,
What thou lovest well is thy true heritage.[18]

NOTES

CHAPTER I: REFLECTIONS ON THE GRAND TOUR

1. Kenner, H. R. H. *A Trip to the Eternal City*. Reprinted from the *Peterborough Review*, late 1898.

2. Aristotle. *Basic Works*. Ed. McKeon. New York: Random House, 1941. 689.

3. Beckford, William. "City of Petrified People." *The Age of the Grand Tour*. Intro. by Anthony Burgess and Francis Haskell. New York: Crown, 1967. 51.

4. Hazlitt, William. "'With Glistering Spires and Pinnacles Adorned.'" *The Age of the Grand Tour*. 56.

5. Ibid., 56.

6. Ibid., 57.

7. Cooper, James Fenimore. "A Reputation for Taste and Intelligence." *The Age of the Grand Tour*. 93.

8. Beckford, Peter. "Comfort, My Good Sir, Is Unknown in Savoy." *The Age of the Grand Tour*. 102.

9.   Boswell, James. *Life of Samuel Johnson*. London: Oxford, 1953. 742.

10. Jameson, Anna. "A First Sight of Rome." *The Age of the Grand Tour*. 117.

11. Stendhal. "The Sacred Capons of the Sistine Chapel." *The Age of the Grand Tour*. 118.

12. Gibbon, Edward. *Autobiography*. London: J. M. Dent, 1948. 122.

13. Ibid., 124.

14. Goethe, Johann Wolfgang von. *Roman Elegies and Other Poems*. Trans. Michael Hamburger. Redding Ridge, CT: Black Swan Books, 1983. V. l. 10.

15. "AE" (Russell, George William). "The Nuts of Knowledge." *Lyrical Poems Old and New*. Dundrum, Dublin: Dun Emer Press, 1903. 4.

16. Kavanagh, Patrick. "Ploughman." *Collected Poems*. London: MacGibbon and Kee, 1968. 3.

17. Joyce, James. *Ulysses*. Ed. H. W. Gabler. New York: Vintage, 1986. Episode IX, l. 213.

18. Milton, John. *Paradise Lost. Complete Poems and Major Prose*. Ed. Merritt Y. Hughes. New York: Odyssey Press, 1957. Book I, ll. 284–91.

19. Ibid., Book XII, ll. 645–49.

20. Wordsworth, William. *The Prelude. Oxford Anthology of English Literature*. Ed. Harold Bloom and Lionel Trilling. Vol. 2. New York: Oxford UP, 1973. Book I, ll. 14–16.

21. Milton, Book I, ll. 756–57.

22. Wordsworth, Book VI, ll. 586–88.

23. Ibid., Book VI, ll. 620–40 (with omissions).

24. Milton, Book V, l. 165.

25. Wordsworth. *Lines Composed a Few Miles Above Tintern Abbey. Oxford Anthology of English Literature*. Lines 93–102.

26. Wordsworth. *The Prelude.* Book IV, ll. 61–63.

CHAPTER II: PORTRAIT OF A MENTOR

1.   Tennyson, Alfred, Lord. *The Princess. Poems.* Ed. C. Ricks. Berkeley: U of California P, 1987. Part 2, l. 355.

2.   Eliot, T. S. "The Love Song of J. Alfred Prufrock," *Complete Poems and Plays.* New York: Harcourt Brace, 1952. Line 1.

3.   Pound. *The Spirit of Romance.* New York: New Directions, n.d. 92.

4.   Pound. "Affirmations, II." *New Age, London.* 14 January 1915. 277.

5.   Pound. *Gaudier-Brzeska, A Memoir.* New York: New Directions, 1960. 86–89.

6.   Pound. *Personae.* New York. Horace Liveright, 1926. 109.

7.   Tennyson. *Morte d'Arthur.* Ed. Ricks. Vol. 2. l. 7.

8.   Kenner, Hugh. *The Pound Era.* Berkeley: U of California P, 1971. 467.

9.   Quoted in Carpenter, Humphrey. *A Serious Character: The Life of Ezra Pound.* Boston: Houghton Mifflin, 1988. 791.

10. Ibid., 792.

11. James, Henry. *The American Scene.* New York: Horizon Press, 1967. 309.

12. Pound. *The Cantos.* New York: New Directions, 1970. Canto I, ll. 3–6.

13. Ibid., Canto I, portions of last 5 lines.

14. Yeats, W. B. "The Fish." *W. B. Yeats: The Poems.* Ed. Richard J. Finneran. New York: Macmillan, 1983. 58.

15. Ibid., 68.

16. Ibid., 80.

17. Paraphrased from Logenbach, James. *Stone Cottage.* New York: Oxford UP, 1988. 19.

18. Eliot. "The Love Song of J. Alfred Prufrock." Lines 62–67.

CHAPTER III: AND I SEE FOR MYSELF

1. James. *Representative Selections*. Ed. L. R. Richardson. New York: American Book Company, 1941. 76.
2. Edel, Leon. *Henry James: The Untried Years*. London: Rupert Hart-Davis, 1953. 122.
3. James. *The American Scene*. 114.
4. Tomlinson, Charles. "Class." *Collected Poems*. New York: Oxford UP, 1985. Lines 1–2.
5. Lewis, Wyndham. *The Mysterious Mr Bull*. London: Robert Hale, 1938. 280.
6. Tomlinson, Charles. "Paring the Apple." *Collected Poems*. 30.
7. Boswell. *Life of Samuel Johnson*. 859.
8. Lewis, Wyndham. "The Sea-Mists of Winter." *The Listener*. British Broadcasting Corporation: May 1951.
9. Ibid.
10. Eliot. "Burnt Norton." *The Four Quartets. Complete Poems and Plays*. Lines 11–14.
11. Williams, William Carlos. *Paterson*. Revised Edition, ed. Christopher MacGowan. New York: New Directions, 1970. 78.
12. Williams. Vol. II. 14.
13. Moore, Marianne. "Bird-Witted." *Collected Poems*. New York: Macmillan/Viking, 1967. 105.
14. Ibid., 106.

CHAPTER IV: THE QUEST FOR THE PAST

1. Pound. *The Cantos*. 447.
2. Tennyson. *Ulysses*. Ed. Ricks. Vol. 1. 618.
3. Kenner, H. R. H. *A Trip to the Eternal City*.
4. Dante. *Inferno. The Portable Dante*. Trans. Laurence Binyon. New York: Viking, 1947. Canto XXXVI, ll. 97–99.
5. Pound. *The Cantos*. 3, ll. 1–9.

CHAPTER V: AND NOW, THE INVISIBLE TOURIST

1. Milton. *Aeropagitica. Complete Poems and Major Prose.* 720.
2. Keats. "On First Looking into Chapman's Homer." *Oxford Anthology of English Literature.* 495, l. 1.
3. *New York Times.* 10 August 1997. 4:3.
4. Martin, Judith. "Miss Manners." *Atlanta Journal/Constitution.* August 1997.
5. Ibid.
6. *Atlanta Journal/Constitution.* 12 August 1997. D:1
7. Ibid.
8. Ibid.
9. Husted, Bill. *Atlanta Journal/Constitution.* 5 August 1997. D: 1.
10. Manguel, Alberto. *Times Literary Supplement.* 4 July 1997. 9.
11. Wordsworth. *The Prelude.* Book VI, ll. 620–40 (with omissions).
12. Wordsworth. "I Wandered Lonely as a Cloud." *Oxford Anthology of English Literature.* 109, l. 17.
13. Quoted in the *Times Literary Supplement.* 4 July 1997. 32.
14. Wordsworth. *Lines Composed a Few Miles Above Tintern Abbey. Oxford Anthology of English Literature.* 149, ll. 95–102.
15. Shakespeare, William. *Cymbeline. Complete Works.* Ed. G. L. Kittredge. Boston: Ginn and Company, 1936. IV. ii: 262–63.
16. Joyce. *Ulysses.* Gabler Edition. New York: Vintage, 1986. Episode VIII, ll. 638–39.
17. Budgen, Frank. *James Joyce and the Making of Ulysses.* 2nd edition. London: Grayson and Grayson, 1937. 20.
18. Pound. *The Cantos.* 521.

ACKNOWLEDGEMENTS

This book was originally developed as a set of Massey Lectures, produced by CBC Radio's *Ideas*. The author is grateful to John Fraser, Master of Massey College at the University of Toronto, and Martha Sharpe, editor of House of Anansi Press, as well as to Bernie Lucht, executive producer of *Ideas*, and Sara Wolch, producer, for the endless trouble they took over its details.

The CBC Massey Lectures Series

Also available from House of Anansi Press in this prestigious series:

The Unconscious Civilization
John Ralston Saul
0-88784-586X (p) $14.95

On the Eve of the Millennium
Conor Cruise O'Brien
0-88784-5592 (p) $12.95

Democracy on Trial
Jean Bethke Elshtain
0-88784-5452 (p) $11.95

*Twenty-First Century
Capitalism*
Robert Heilbroner
0-88784-5347 (p) $11.95

The Malaise of Modernity
Charles Taylor
0-88784-5207 (p) $11.95

Biology as Ideology
R. C. Lewontin
0-88784-5185 (p) $11.95

*Prisons We Choose to Live
Inside*
Doris Lessing
0-88784-5215 (p) $9.95

The Politics of the Family
R. D. Laing
0-88784-5460 (p) $8.95

Nostalgia for the Absolute
George Steiner
0-88784-5940 (p) $17.95

Necessary Illusions
Noam Chomsky
0-88784-5746 (p) $19.95

Compassion and Solidarity
Gregory Baum
0-88784-5320 (p) $11.95

The Real World of Democracy
C. B. Macpherson
0-88784-5304 (p) $9.95

Latin America
Carlos Fuentes
0-88784-146X (p) $8.95

The Real World of Technology
Ursula Franklin
0-88784-5312 (p) $9.95

The Educated Imagination
Northrop Frye
0-88784-5983 (p) $12.95

Designing Freedom
Stafford Beer
0-88784-5479 (p) $10.95